We Speak for Ourselves

We Speak for Ourselves

EXPERIENCES IN HOMOSEXUAL COUNSELLING

Jack Babuscio

LONDON

SPCK

First published 1976
SPCK
Holy Trinity Church
Marylebone Road
London NW1 4DU

Printed in Great Britain by
The Camelot Press Ltd, Southampton
ISBN 0 281 02963 6

To GLF and London FRIEND

Acknowledgements

Thanks are due to the following for permission to quote from copyright sources:

American Journal of Psychotherapy: 'Psychotherapy Today or Where Do We Go From Here?' by Carl R. Rogers, in the *American Journal of Psychotherapy*, January 1963

Angus & Robertson (U.K.) Ltd and Outerbridge & Lazard, Inc: *Homosexual: Oppression and Liberation* by Dennis Altman

The Campaign for Homosexual Equality: *Comments on Manifesto 7*, a Report prepared by the London West End Group of the Campaign for Homosexual Equality

The Gay Academics Union, Inc.: 'Coming Out' by Howard J. Brown, in *The Universities and the Gay Experience: A Conference Sponsored by the Men and Women of the Gay Academics Union, 23 and 24 November 1973*

RT Collective (*RT: A Journal of Radical Therapy*): 'Surviving Psychotherapy' by Christopher Z. Hobson, in *Rough Times*, ed. Jerome Agel

St Martin's Press, Inc: *Society and the Healthy Homosexual* by George Weinberg.

Chapter 3, 'Passing through Oppression', is based on an article entitled 'Passing for Straight: The Politics of the Closet', which originally appeared in *Gay News*, No. 62. The author is grateful to *Gay News* for permission to use this material.

Contents

Preface

The title of this book speaks for a new generation of homosexuals, one concerned with probing the creative possibilities of being gay in the present rather than locating the causes of homosexuality in the past.

It has never been my aim in writing *We Speak for Ourselves* to pursue any particular counselling theory or to suggest interviewing techniques for use in counselling situations. Such information can readily be found elsewhere. But it has been my wish to allow gay men and women to explore the personal and social implications of their own situations and in their own words. Such an approach, I believe, will serve the purpose of widening the reader's understanding of what it means to be gay by demonstrating through example the ways in which attitudes to sexuality can affect gay relationships and influence aspirations towards a fuller and happier life.

In reading this book, the reader will bear in mind that no one homosexual or group of homosexuals can speak for all homosexuals, any more than one heterosexual or group of heterosexuals can speak for all heterosexuals. Each individual represented in these pages speaks for him or her self alone. No one claims to be, or is presented as, a representative of a type.

One thing most contributors do have in common, however, is a deep awareness of the important place that homosexuality has had in their lives. This consciousness is evident in much of what they say, and it reflects, at least in part, the individual and group counselling situations in which most have been involved.

The material in this book, reproduced here with the full consent of all contributors, consists primarily of edited transcriptions of tape-recordings, but also of letters and personal statements submitted to me at my request. Names, places, and minor details have been altered in every instance, with the exception of those few accounts which have already been published elsewhere. This determination to protect the anonymity of individuals, I would add, reflects my own wish to respect the privacy of all those concerned.

JACK BABUSCIO

London 1976

1
What are the Problems?

'We only become what we are by the radical and deep-seated refusal of that which others have made of us.'—Jean-Paul Sartre, preface to Frantz Fanon's *The Wretched of the Earth* (1961)

An Urgent Word to the Counsellor

This book is intended for all those who counsel others and who care about the quality of that counselling. It is for the professional and the non-professional alike—for anyone, in short, who gives help to those who seek understanding and assistance in living their lives. Counsellors are, in this broad sense, help-givers. They are parents and friends, teachers and clergy, nurses and psychologists, you and I. People, in other words, to whom others feel they can come and talk.

But counselling involves more than simply listening. Those who help others are also agents of change, modifying the feelings and attitudes of individuals, as well as their social situations. Often, such people feel inadequate to their task when confronted with a homosexual. At such times they bemoan their inadequate knowledge or their lack of qualifications in psychology, deciding, in the end, to refer this 'problem' to a 'specialist' in the field, or, failing that, to someone who has earned a reputation for being 'good with such people'. These counsellors, in particular, will find this book useful, for it has been my intention throughout to share with the reader what I have found to be most helpful and practical in my own counselling experience with homosexuals.

As the reader is already aware, the past decade has been marked by a growing wave of public attention to all the varieties of human sexual behaviour. Unfortunately, most of the growth has been in volume rather than quality. As far as homosexuality is concerned, the preoccupation with aetiology, on the one hand, and the 'exotic' aspects of the subject, on the other, continues unabated. Almost totally neglected is what, in fact, we most need: a good counselling guide that can provide information and advice on the problems arising out of homosexual adaptations.

It is important, when we speak of homosexuality, to remember that we are dealing with very substantial numbers of men and women from all social groups. Using the Kinsey Institute statistics[1] and the recent cross-cultural studies of Martin Weinberg and Colin Williams of the (Indiana) Institute for Sex Research,[2] we find that, on average, ten per cent of the entire adult population is predominantly homosexual. Even those who reject such high figures as these are confronted with the fact that no source estimates the incidence of homosexuality as being less than one in twenty—five per cent of the total population. Opting for the very lowest figure available, this means that, in terms of numbers, there are some two million adults in the UK who are predominantly attracted to their own sex. If we are to include the even greater number of people who have at least some personal involvement in homosexuality, or who are attracted to both sexes, the figures will be very much higher.

Taking into account the social context in which the homosexual lives, many of these more than two million gay people will be confused and troubled by their sexual orientation. For despite the recent upsurge in publicity and discussion, there remains little genuine acceptance of homosexuality as a valid sexual and social lifestyle. Many may wish to join the 'permissive' age, but few, in fact, are ready for it. As a boy in his early twenties remarked to a journalist who had accompanied the Gay Liberation Front in its 1973 march up Oxford Street: 'Try wearing a *Glad to be Gay* button for a day or so, and see for yourself just how permissive people really are.'

Indeed, in some respects our less inhibited references to homosexuality appear to have actually intensified fears and prejudices. Inhibitions and feelings of guilt are often exacerbated in those very people who have been awakened to their true sexual identity by the recent storm of publicity. In its relentless exposure of everything that departs from the statistical norm, the media have made *voyeurs* of us all; they have not necessarily made us more accepting of the legitimacy of the sexual variations which they describe in such graphic detail.

All the same, increased publicity on behalf of sexual minorities has important implications for the counsellor. Today's help-givers find themselves confronted with ever-increasing numbers of people who are able to identify their homosexual component. Not all these people, though, can cope with their discovery. 'The love that dare not speak its name' may have found its tongue, but self-acceptance is more difficult to come by. The journey from the 'closet' to the 'street' is often long and painful, and the counsellor must understand the special nature of the problems that the traveller faces. It is not enough to be an unbiased and sympathetic listener, important though this is. Counsellors need to know, as best they can, what it is like to be 'different', to bear a stigma, in a frequently hostile world.

Those of us who care to help people in distress should be alarmed, then, by the findings of a recent working party set up by a national Conference on Social Needs to study counselling services for homosexuals. It was the carefully considered view of its members that only a limited number of agencies were either willing or able to offer help. The vast majority of these were centred in London, though, in fact, the needs of homosexuals are frequently greater in the provinces, especially in remote country areas where effective help is often virtually unobtainable. Most other agencies and professional workers, 'though apparently sympathetic, felt daunted by the subject and therefore did nothing'. On the basis of all the available evidence, the working party 'reluctantly' concluded that there remained as late as 1973 'a considerable lack of knowledge of, and interest in, the needs of homosexuals'.[3]

The need is therefore obvious, and *urgent*. Counsellors are required who can and will be of help to the large numbers of gay people neglected by our social services. For all too many, the pain of loneliness and social isolation remains as acute as ever, and these burdens are scarcely made lighter when some sections of the community to whom we traditionally turn for help in our emotional and spiritual lives show only apathy, when understanding and acceptance are required.

But first the counsellor needs to be aware of his or her own position with regard to homosexuality. We are dealing here with a psychosexual orientation which rouses strong and often contradictory feelings in people. It is imperative, if we have the interest of those we would help at heart, that we carefully examine our conscience to ascertain the extent to which the available evidence may have coloured our attitude. So much of the published literature on the subject has tended, until very recently, to regard homosexuality *per se* as a problem. This is as true of the subjective-confessional autobiographies of homosexuals as it is of the sensationalist fiction that purports to explore the so-called 'tragic twilight world' of the homosexual. But it is even more true of the descriptive and analytical accounts which view homosexuality from the position of the outsider. These historical, psychiatric, sociological, legal, theological, and medical studies are usually concerned with the aetiology or social impact of what their authors regard as socially destructive, neurotic, deviant, criminal, sinful, or sick behaviour.

This book grows out of a disillusionment with such works, the theory and discussion of which is rarely grounded in the problems and situations of real people. And it is this fact, more than any other, that has led me to write a guide for counsellors who work, or who will in future work, with homosexuals. I have therefore attempted in these chapters to present a world that will be recognizable to those who live in it, rather than those who briefly tour it; and to demonstrate that such problems as do exist for the homosexual—and it is my intention to allow gay people to define these problems for themselves, and in their own words—spring from negative societal reacion to homosexuality' rather than from anything inherent in the homosexual orientation itself. In short, my aim is to provide as many insights as possible into the multifarious ways in which gay people view their status as citizens of a world whose institutions are designed to meet not their needs, but those of the heterosexual majority.

The Problem of Identity

Because attention has been focused almost exclusively on the *causes* of homosexuality, the *creative* aspects of this sexual variation have been largely ignored. This, of course, is understandable. So long as homosexuality is regarded as a sexual orientation in need of alteration or 'cure', there can be little concern for the creative process of self-actualization—the growth towards psychological maturity, the realization of individual potential, and the development of fulfilling relationships.

No matter how compassionate or well-intentioned the researcher, it is none the less a fact that any investigation into the aetiology of homosexuality will be biased from the outset unless the search is broadened to encompass the whole field of human sexuality. In other words, to consider only the question 'What causes homosexuality?' without also asking the parallel question 'What causes heterosexuality?' is to make a value judgement in favour of the latter. Heterosexual behaviour is thus taken to be the norm—an unquestioned assumption which determines the selection of evidence, colours the interpretation of facts, and ensures a conclusion that does scant justice to gay people.

It is as a direct result of society's failure to accept homosexuality as a legitimate variation of the sexual drive that the gay person's principal problem becomes one of finding an acceptable identity within a hostile environment. Yet this search for a satisfying self-image is often thwarted by a barrier of demeaning myths and stereotypes which still surround the issue of homosexuality. Consider, for example, the story of **Claude**, thirty-eight, who, as a young man, consulted the literature of homosexuality—'analytical, fictional, and confessional'—in the hope of finding some acceptable sense of self-as-homosexual:

> You can't name a book that I didn't consult. And in each of them the message rang out loud and clear: you're a criminal, and your crime is against God, nature, society, yourself.
> As I talk to you I wonder what on earth made me persevere. I think, perhaps, because one *must* know *who* one is, and *why* one is different. And as homosexuality was not, in those days, something you dared discuss in polite conversation, one consulted the 'experts'. And this is what I did. I read everything I could get my hands on. But the literature was uniformly negative. How well I remember those *thousands* of case studies shrouded in gloom and doom, all written in

plaintive tones of guilt and self-hatred. I wanted to cry aloud after reading them. The unhappy homosexual! Sentenced to 'life' for the crime of being gay. How ironic that word, 'gay', seemed to me then. . . .
I began to look upon the straight world with envy and sorrow. The heterosexual inhabited a kind of golden world from which I was for ever excluded. I felt very much an alien. It's rather like the title of that book, *Invisible Man*. That's how I felt, like an invisible man.

It is very difficult to feel good about oneself when so little of a positive nature is said about one's own kind. Since the sense of self is in large part determined by an individual's perception of his or her social role, popular stereotypes and social expectations are liable to count for a great deal in the development of the gay person's self-concept. This can be seen in the story of **Martin**, twenty-four:

The problem I was faced with years ago, when I first realized I was gay, was learning to like myself. This isn't easy when people think of you as sick or immature.
Before I even knew I was homosexual, I remember my school friends talking about the 'pooves'. When finally I realized I was '*one of them*', you can imagine how I felt. . . .
I fought my homosexuality for a long time. I'd persuade myself that I couldn't be *entirely* gay since I didn't behave like the stereotyped gays they joke about on telly, or that you see in films.
Eventually, though, I couldn't deny it any longer. That is, I couldn't deny it *to myself*. I still laughed along with the others when 'queer jokes' were told. I hated myself afterwards, and also felt disloyal. And, of course, all this only aggravated my feelings of guilt.
And yet, I felt it was wiser to say nothing because if all the others felt this way about homosexuals, there must be some good reason. And I *didn't* want to lose my friends. . . . There were *so many* risks in being open. So I kept my homosexuality a secret for as long as I could.

As this story suggests, the self-admitted homosexual is not necessarily a self-accepting one. In fact, at some point or other in their lives many gays have tried, like Martin, to deny their gayness, and with fairly predictable results.

As Christopher Z. Hobson has said, in an essay entitled 'Surviving Psychotherapy':[4]

> In my teens I tried actively not to be homosexual. Even when I stopped trying, at twenty-two, I didn't accept being gay—I merely decided to express it until something changed, because I realized that in trying not to love men, I was losing the ability to love at all. Not until I was twenty-five did I begin to see homosexuality as something that shouldn't be despised, and not until I was twenty-eight—only one year ago—did I 'come out' in the sense of beginning to live openly as a homosexual. Only then, moreover, did I actively step into gay life and begin to meet other gay people. During those fourteen years I had almost no sexual contacts and was, naturally, unhappy, frustrated, and confused.

The Stigma of Homosexuality

So long as significant numbers of people refuse to accept homosexuality as a legitimate variety of sexual expression, many gays will continue to fear the consequences of being open. The counsellor must therefore not be surprised to learn that even in this 'permissive' age there still exist homosexuals who, like Martin, and Christopher Hobson, refuse to put at risk their friendships, reputation, or general well-being by 'coming out', or being open, to their family and friends. After all, our society is one in which everyone is assumed to be heterosexual until proved otherwise, and the reaction of those who discover the homosexuality of a relative, friend, or colleague is often one of surprise or pain, anger or resentment, and only rarely one of genuine acceptance. 'The tune is called by the heterosexual male', David Blamires has observed; 'it is a world in which . . . his sexual preferences, his fantasies, even, permeate almost every aspect of life.'[5]

Gay people are thus at risk of feeling inferior *not* because of what they do, but, rather, because of the threat which they represent. To summarize briefly this curious logic: homosexual activity is labelled 'deviant'; deviance is perceived as failure-to-conform; nonconformist behaviour is socially proscribed; and the ensuing penalties are rationalized by a philosophy that explains the 'threat' which sexual minorities represent. Thus, homosexuality is, for some, a sin; for others it is 'against nature'; still others regard it as an illness; and, under the law, it may constitute a crime.

There can be few homosexuals who have not believed at some time or other in their lives the validity of one or more of these damaging stereotypes: sinful, unnatural, sick, criminal: Tina, for example, is a young, recently divorced mother of a seven-year-old son who once lived 'in constant fear of succumbing, some day, to the temptation of loving another woman':

I don't know that my religious upbringing was any more strict than that of most girls my age. I took a keen interest in church affairs, though. All of the social events in our village that I was permitted to attend were church affairs.

My most vivid recollections of these gatherings is that they seemed to be dress rehearsals for marriage—learning how to be wives and mothers, or husbands and fathers. Perhaps that's unfair, but that's how I remember them. . . .

Then, of course, Mother would always speak of my future in terms of a home and a family. 'Now, when you're married, dear', she'd say, or, 'When you have children', or 'Your husband' this, and 'Your husband' that. . . . It made me think of the family as part of some grand design and I felt, who am I to upset everyone's plans for me? Yet I couldn't generate even the slightest enthusiasm for the prospect of one day being a wife, mother, homemaker. . . . I was very confused by my attitude. I seemed, to myself, unique.

When I was about fifteen I began to experience 'feelings' for other girls. I felt very guilty about this. It was quite bad enough thinking about *boys* in that way. It was positively *evil* to have these feelings for girls. Still, two and two didn't yet add up to 'lesbian'. I was learning, though, what it means to be different, and to feel isolated.

One night I remember I couldn't sleep because a close friend, someone towards whom I felt very close, for whom I had very warm feelings (and who, I think, felt the same way about me), suddenly moved up north. I was despondent! I wanted to die, I felt so suddenly alone.

At about two o'clock in the morning, I was still awake. I put my robe on and started down to the kitchen. But when I came into the hall I saw the light was on in my parents' room. I could hear them talking in hushed voices. It was something to do with this girl who had 'disgraced' herself with a woman who was lodging in her parents' home. I heard my mother say, in the voice she generally reserved for sinners, 'There's a special place in hell for *those* women. . . .' Our parish priest apparently agreed, because on the following Sunday his sermon was full of oblique references to the affair, and these were 'spiced' with quotations from the Scriptures. Leviticus, I think. . . .

I suppose the more sophisticated knew precisely what the old fellow was on about, but I was much too naïve. A friend later explained it to me: '*Lesbians*', she said. And that was all.

The next day I went to the library and checked the dictionaries. After reading the entry for 'lesbian', I was in a panic. I imagined all of hell's devils pointing at me. I was in no doubt now. My feelings had branded me a sinner.

It is very easy to minimize the extent of suffering experienced by individuals who imagine their faith to be in conflict with their homosexuality. Counsellors should keep Tina's story in mind, then. For although Tina is today convinced that Christianity and homosexuality are compatible, it was not so long ago that feelings of guilt and shame, based on the conviction of being a sinner, were, for her, a source of considerable anguish. Counsellors concerned to help those with this particular conflict are advised to look carefully at Chapter 5.

An even more frequently encountered charge than 'sinner' is one which says that homosexuality is 'against the laws of nature'. **Derek**, nineteen, still regards his gayness as a form of perversion:

It's unnatural, isn't it? Nature never intended two blokes to have sex, did it? . . . It would be a right old world if everyone was like us. There wouldn't be anybody left! The world would die off. . . . It's just not natural! What about kids? Why were we made the way we are, different sexes, if it weren't natural, you know, to have kids? . . .

I don't know. I wish I was wrong. I really do, because . . .

most of the time, I feel like a freak inside . . . and I guess that's
what I am, too: a freak. . . .

Although the argument that homosexuality is 'unnatural' has
no rational standing, it is none the less a seductive one to the
popular imagination. Hardly surprising, then, that some gays,
like Derek, have successfully internalized its surface plausibility
and regard themselves as 'freaks'. My advice to counsellors who
attempt to deal with this 'nature argument' is to be first quite
certain that they understand it themselves. Generally speaking,
people who claim that homosexuality is 'unnatural' are, in
effect, asserting that: (a) nature did not intend two men or two
women to enjoy sex together, as the function of sex is
reproduction; (b) the structure and function of the sexual
organs are determined by nature and must not be 'perverted' by
man.

Let us briefly consider these assertions, each of which assumes
that a law of nature embodies observable and repeatable
phenomena acting in a certain way and under a specific set of
conditions. Two examples of such 'natural laws' would be: (1)
humans cannot fly, and (2) there is pain during childbirth. Now
to say that something is against the laws of nature means that the
laws of nature must not be altered. Yet in both the examples
given above man has, in fact, modified the 'laws' of nature.
Hence, the law which says that humans cannot fly has been
bypassed by the laws of aerodynamics. As far as birth pains are
concerned, we should not forget that less than a century ago
people passionately argued either (a) that nature had not
intended to make conception painless, or (b) that God intended
women to suffer pain in childbirth because of Eve's sin: 'In
sorrow thou shalt bring forth children' (Gen. 3.16). Yet how
many among today's clergy would protest against the
administration of sedatives for use by expectant mothers on the
grounds that this is an obvious subversion of the 'laws' of
nature? I believe that few, if any, would do this.

In short, there is nothing within nature itself that can possibly
serve as a criterion for the modification of its 'laws'. Man is a
creative being, constantly correcting his ethical insights and
altering his universe into something better that will give added
meaning to his life. Nature cannot be the guide for man's

actions; it is man who must impose upon nature his own dreams and values.

As for Derek's assertion that the race would become extinct if homosexuality were the norm ('The world would die off. . . .'), even this is no longer (if ever it was) a tenable contribution to our argument. It assumes, first, that the only valid function of sex is procreation and, second, that those who do not choose to procreate are socially irresponsible. If this were so, we would then need to consider such questions as: 'Is celibacy unnatural?' 'What would happen if we all took the vow of chastity, as many clergy do?' 'Is it unnatural to have sex purely for pleasure, rather than for procreation?' 'Must women remain celibate after their menopause?' 'Should we advise heterosexuals who cannot have children to abstain from sex?'

What the counsellor needs to emphasize is that sex for pleasure is neither undesirable nor 'unnatural'. Sex reaches into the total texture of our lives, and for this reason alone it must be valued as a road to loving relationships. This is the point to stress, and though it may not put an immediate end to all anxieties and doubts, it can be an important first step along the road to self-acceptance for gays like Derek.

Another stereotype used to discredit gays is that which says: homosexuals are sick and therefore deserve our pity. **Peter**, a post-graduate student, speaks here of his rejection of the 'sick' label during the course of his two years of psychotherapy:

It's very strange that if gays are, as they say, 'psychologically sick', then it's always traced back to the fact of their being homosexual. But if heterosexuals are 'sick' in this way, it can be attributed to unknown factors; no one says to them, 'You're sick because you're heterosexual.'
Funnily enough, it was my therapist who made me realize that being gay didn't automatically mean 'being sick'. I'm sure this wasn't his intention, but several things he said started me to think. At one of our sessions, he expressed an opinion that confirmed bachelors were 'disturbed' because they 'feared' marriage and women. Later, at another session, he remarked that some psychiatrists, himself included, firmly held to the opinion that a belief in God was a symptom of autistic behaviour, 'a dangerous absorption in fantasy'. In effect he

was saying that prayer is a form of magic, and that those who pray are unable to face reality—they're 'disturbed'.

This shattered me, and I asked him at another session if he meant what he said. He was obviously a bit bothered with himself for having said *anything*. He also seemed a bit concerned by my interpretation, but he stood by all he said.

By his logic, then, I was sick for being homosexual and unmarried, but healthy because I'm an agnostic. It was then that I asked myself who exactly is it that says I'm sick? Who determines how you define normal, healthy behaviour? It's a legitimate question because standards differ. Take the Soviet Union, for example, where political nonconformity is often defined as mental illness . . . it's difficult to avoid the conclusion that mental health is measured according to how well you conform to what the majority think and do.

It is a rather daunting task to consider the crimes committed throughout history in the interests of protecting the 'health' of the individual and of society. As far as homosexuality is concerned, those who think of gays as ill are, as Peter implies, positing heterosexuality as the norm. Yet most informed opinion of recent origin has rejected this assumption. Indeed, in 1974, the members of the American Psychiatric Association, after assessing the matter in the most rigorous diagnostic and statistical terms, overwhelmingly concluded that homosexuality could not be considered a form of personality disturbance or mental breakdown, i.e. that homosexuality, of itself, does not regularly cause subjective distress, nor is it regularly associated with any generalized impairment in social effectiveness.

Many of us, awed by science, sometimes forget that psychological theories about the nature of man are not universally accepted truths but, rather, *partial* versions of the truth put forward by people whose ideas are often diametrically opposed. Facts do not 'speak for themselves'; they are interpreted by human beings. And human beings are not in total agreement about what constitutes illness. In fact, there is considerable disagreement on this point within the therapeutic profession itself. As Professor Carl Rogers, the founder of the client-centred approach to psychotherapy, has said:[6]

Our differences as therapists do not lie simply in attaching different levels to the same phenomenon. . . . We differ at the most basic levels of our personal experience. . . . We are not agreed on whether the goal is removal of symptoms, reorganization of personality, curing of disease, or adjustment. . . . A one-sentence summary would be: The field of psychotherapy is in a mess. Therapists are not in agreement as to their goals or aims. . . . They are in deep disagreement as to the theoretical structure which contains their work. They cannot agree as to whether a given experience for a client is healing or destructive, growth-producing or damaging. They cannot agree as to what constitutes failure. They diverge sharply in their views as to the promising directions for the future. It seems as though the field is completely chaotic and divided.

In addition to the labels 'sin', 'unnatural', and 'sick', certain sexual acts performed by homosexuals, legal in the case of heterosexuals, are regarded by the law as 'criminal'. This particular form of discrimination will be considered at some length in Chapter 3. For the time being it is sufficient to point out that serious problems can arise from the fact that the age of consent for homosexuals is twenty-one, whereas heterosexuals are considered adults (for the purposes of sexual activity) by the age of sixteen.

Mike, nineteen, talks about what he regards as the principal problem of being labelled 'criminal' in consequence of one's sexual preferences:

Let's say that you're straight and between the ages of sixteen and twenty-one. If you're having relationship problems with the opposite sex, you can go to people and talk about it. Books and films tell you how to behave, what you should do in certain situations, where you can go when you need help. Now if you're gay, there's nothing of the kind. In the first place, you're supposed to be celibate till the age of twenty-one. And if you're not, you had better keep it quiet. Another thing is that people are afraid of giving advice. They are afraid of running foul of the law. You can't advertise social activities for under-twenty-ones, because this can put you in trouble with the law, too—it may be thought an incitement to criminal activity. . . .

All this limits your opportunities for meeting other gays of your own age. It means you're slow to develop gay relationships. And the longer it takes, the more difficult it becomes. It's not easy to get a good relationship going if you've had so little practice doing it.

The law says no sex till you're twenty-one! Can you imagine making that demand on hets? They wouldn't stand for it! I'd say this attitude on the part of the law has made me fairly cynical of our system of justice.

Speaking for myself, though, I can't say that the law has inhibited me in any noticeable way. Perhaps you feel a bit more 'brave' at university. And then, too, there's Gay Soc. . . . No, I'd say I don't ever *think* of the law as far as sex is concerned.

But that's not true for everyone I know. I know guys of my own age who literally cut themselves off. They're afraid to get close to someone else . . . and I know that this springs, at least in part, from the legal situation. Inside, you know you're a lawless person. This is bound to affect your outward behaviour.

Mike's point about the way in which relationships are inhibited by the internal knowledge of one's lawlessness suggests another way in which society's negative attitudes restrict the growth of personality. When gays are discouraged from expressing their feelings of tenderness and affection—feelings regarded as healthy when directed towards the opposite sex—then progress towards positive self-identification is once again thwarted. Thus, for Peter Wildeblood, author of *Against the Law*, it proved impossible to be a self-accepting homosexual while living a conventional life in English society. The internal knowledge of being a lawless person was, in fact, the start of a split existence, the double lifestyle of the 'passing' homosexual:[7]

I was forced to be deceitful, living one life during my working hours and another when I was free. I had two sets of friends; almost, one might say, two faces. At the back of my mind there was always a nagging fear that my two worlds might suddenly collide . . . it was necessary to watch every word I spoke, and every gesture that I made in case I gave myself away.

The Human Consequences of Social Pressures

The stereotypes outlined above will only matter if gays accept them as being true to themselves. 'It is thus with most of us,' says Eric Hoffer, 'we are what other people say we are. We know ourselves chiefly by hearsay.'[8] Once the labels 'sinner', 'unnatural', 'sick', and 'criminal' are internalized, feelings of guilt and shame are thus the inevitable result. Such feelings can then adversely affect all of one's relationships, particularly with regard to one's parents. Mothers and fathers often sense the existence of a 'problem', yet remain silent, and then are hurt that their children should not trust them sufficiently to share their worries. **Ralph**, twenty, is a case in point:

My parents knew something was wrong when I dropped out of university. They couldn't understand this as my grades had always been well above average. . . .

At university I worked hard at fighting my homosexuality. In time, I became very tense. I found I couldn't concentrate on my studies. Finally, in mid-term, I dropped everything.

I returned to Nottingham, made plans to get a job and save some money, then maybe go to Canada.

My parents were really confused. But they thought, well, he's got this problem that he wants to keep to himself; okay, let's see how it goes, but stay with us, you can save more money that way, then make up your mind later.

Weeks and then months went by, and they noticed that I was becoming more and more distant with people, *and* with them. The truth is that their presence made me feel uneasy. There was this unspoken thing between us, so that we couldn't be in a room together without an argument.

There was frustration on all sides. . . . Maybe theirs was in some ways worse. I don't know. My father becomes angry when he can't express his feelings in words. He's never had much of an education himself, and he's always wanted me to have a good one.

. . . Sometimes they'd try and guess what was bothering me. They'd say, 'Is it a girl? Let us know if it's a girl, because we'll

try and understand. Please trust us.' And I'd probably snap
back something like, 'No, it's *not* a girl, now please leave me
alone.' And this, you know, would only make my father more
upset, while my mother would go on about her being 'of no
use whatsoever'. . . .
All of which had the effect of making me want to crawl into a
deep hole, cover myself up with dirt, and just stay
underground for ever.

When people like Ralph are unable to find constructive outlets
for their feelings of guilt and shame, there is always the
possibility that eventually they may project such feelings on to
others like themselves. And this is one of the principal reasons
why some gays have such difficulty in developing relationships
beyond the casual stage, a problem discussed at greater length in
Chapter 7.

The social isolation which Ralph and others have described is,
in fact, one of the most frequently encountered causes of
unhappiness and suffering for homosexuals who seek the help
of a counsellor. Many, having successfully insulated themselves
for years against all but the most superficial contacts, will find it
extremely difficult, if not impossible, to relate to other gays in an
undefended way. Such a legacy of repression is particularly hard
to overcome in the case of older homosexuals. The guilt and
inhibitions which lead to early social withdrawal may take a high
toll in terms of a person's psychological well-being. The present
older generation, having been conditioned to be shy and
secretive, does not have the freedom of approach currently
enjoyed by many younger gays. **Phil**, sixty-seven, has just moved
into a local authority home. He attempts here to define some of
the problems confronting older gays:

The older homosexuals were forced to lie. There wasn't much
of a choice. Lie and survive: that's the story. And now we're
paying the penalty.
Some of the younger ones don't like to hear this. They haven't
lived through the sort of days people like me did. They don't
understand. They expect you to be always positive about
things, to be brave and militant. They don't want to be
depressed by your sad stories of days-gone-by. . . .
Yes, I am bitter. People think your need for love dies, at latest,

by the age of sixty. There's a greater need for companionship at my age. . . . I would like to be in touch with other homosexuals of my age group. But there are problems when you're older—distances, for example, or time and costs.
Older people are often much more stable and loyal than the young. I wish more people could understand.

The process of ageing can be stressful and problematic for all people, regardless of sexual orientation. But as gay relationships involve none of the legal supports that keep heterosexual marriages intact, older homosexuals are often depicted as lonely, isolated, and unable to maintain active social involvement with other gays. Thus, the 'folk view' often portrays the ageing homosexual as, in the words of one commentator, 'so desperately lonely and frightened . . . that he frantically beats the walls in his anguish'.[9]

It would help the counsellor to balance this traditional perception of the older homosexual's psychological problems with that of recent studies on the subject. Data collected by Weinberg and Williams, for example, strenuously contradict the folk view outlined above. 'We find', say the authors,[10]

no age-related differences in self-acceptance, anxiety, depression, or loneliness. In fact, our data suggest that in some respects our older homosexuals have greater well-being than our younger homosexuals.

Why this wide discrepancy between the two views? The most likely answer, it seems to me, is that many commentators will impute to older gays their own perspectives and expectations, thus concluding that the social situation of the older homosexual is unenviable. What such commentators fail to percieve, however, is that people can, and do, adapt in a positive manner to the realistic possibilities of their socio-sexual situation.

This is not to suggest, of course, that the situation of older gays is without problems. Some aspects of the 'folk view' can certainly be supported, as Phil's story suggests. Thus, older homosexuals tend to have fewer social contacts within the gay scene; they visit pubs and clubs less frequently; they are far more likely to be living alone; they may be faced with socio-legal problems such as inheritance, taxation, and insurance.

On the other hand, there are tentative steps being taken to
alleviate the isolation and loneliness of elderly gays such as Phil.
As far as providing social contacts is concerned, Icebreakers,
FRIEND, and CHE's highly successful social groups are now
arranging meetings in a new sort of atmosphere, one largely free
of the tension and sexual barter so characteristic of the
commercial pub, club, and disco scene. These gay lib meetings
are providing opportunities for homosexual men and women of
all ages to meet socially without the usual automatic sexual
motives being read into simple acts of friendliness and concern.
(A list of such gay groups can be found on pp. 136–43.)

Much more can still be done, of course, and CHE's
'Comments on *Manifesto 7*', which deals with the emotional
needs of the retired and elderly gay, makes two constructive
suggestions:[11]

> Local Authorities and others who run old people's homes
> must seriously consider the needs of the homosexuals who
> may be admitted to their establishments. The problems of the
> older homosexual differ in kind, though not in degree, from
> those of heterosexuals and must attract different solutions. At
> the moment these problems are dealt with inside a
> heterosexual framework. . . .
> Finally, we should all realize that although . . . we have
> referred to the problem of the elderly homosexual, it would
> be truer to say that it is the problem of *our* attitude to him or
> her that needs to be considered. Although it is proper to
> initiate research and carry out practical aid programmes, it
> must be borne in mind that ultimately our reaction as
> individuals to the elderly homosexuals that we meet is of
> greater importance.

Summary

In this chapter I have defined the counsellor as an agent of social
change, as well as someone offering help to those seeking
understanding and assistance in the conduct of their lives.

Most homosexuals lead quite happy and satisfied lives.
However, there are those who do require help from outside
their immediate circle of family and friends. It is here that the

counsellor can be of use in helping to alleviate the loneliness and isolation which, for all too many, remain as acute as ever.

Finding an acceptable identity has been isolated as the principal problem confronting the homosexual (**Claude, Martin**). This problem is a direct result of society's failure to accept homosexuality as a legitimate variation of the sexual drive. The gay person's search for an acceptable self-image is, in turn, thwarted by a barrier of stereotypes: 'sinner' (**Tina**), 'unnatural' (**Derek**), 'sick' (**Peter**), and 'criminal' (**Mike**). These stereotypes can, if successfully internalized, result in feelings of guilt and shame that will adversely affect one's relationships (**Ralph**).

Those who have isolated themselves from others in this way may, in time, find it extremely difficult to relate to other gays in an undefended way. The legacy of repression is particularly difficult to overcome in the case of older gays (**Phil**). However, counsellors are advised to balance the traditional folk view of the ageing homosexual with that of recent research which suggests that in some respects older gays have greater well-being than younger homosexuals.

2
On Being Different

'To be nobody-but-myself—in a world which is doing its best, night and day, to make you everybody else—means to fight the hardest battle which any human being can fight, and never stop fighting.'—e. e. cummings, quoted in Charles Norman's *The Magic-Maker* (1958)

Most people find it difficult to justify their aggressive behaviour or intolerant attitudes unless they are first able, in some way or other, to dehumanize their victims. 'Every society', Nietzsche once observed, 'has a tendency to reduce its "opponents" to caricatures.'[1] Hence, blacks are 'niggers'; the police are 'pigs'; politicians of a right-wing hue are 'fascists'; students are 'hippies'; judges speak of certain categories of defendant as 'monsters'; gays are labelled 'sinner', 'unnatural', 'sick', and 'criminal'. Such stereotypes, because they are dismissive of individual differences within particular groups, are not only cruelly unfair and potentially destructive of self-esteem; they can, in addition, be self-fulfilling prophecies.

One means of reversing this process of intolerance and dehumanization is through empathy—the capacity to participate in another person's feelings or ideas. This basic *human* skill is of great importance to the counsellor, particularly to the *non-gay* counsellor, for it helps one to respond to others as *people*, rather than as *problems*. Unless we are able to place ourselves in someone else's shoes, it may well be impossible to understand the thoughts and emotions of others whose experiences and lifestyles are sometimes very different from our own.

This empathetic quality doesn't necessarily lead to attraction, of course. In other words, I may feel I understand you, yet still not care to have you as a friend. But empathy should facilitate mutual understanding and help to eliminate any feelings of intolerance which, try as we may, some of us still find difficult to purge. In this chapter, then, I am asking the reader to consider the question: 'What is it like to be a member of a sexual minority?', and, by way of assistance in reaching an answer, I shall supply the views of those who describe themselves as homosexual, bisexual, paedophile, transvestite, and transsexual.

Sexual Labels

Sexuality remains, even today, a subject shrouded in mystery, controversy, and ignorance. Adding to the general confusion are the use of labels to compartmentalize sexual behaviour for the purpose of immediate identification. I shall not dwell here on the ethics of labelling except to say that if labels must be used, they should at least be used with as much caution and precision as possible. For we can never assume, thanks to the popular mythology surrounding sexuality, that another person's understanding of a label or term will even approximately correlate with that of our own.

Take, for example, the term 'homosexual'. Definitions abound, and some of these will be the subject of further exploration below. For now, it is enough to stress the importance of the gay person's definition. It is absolutely essential that counsellors know the way or ways in which homosexuals perceive themselves. One reason for laying such emphasis on this might be illustrated by reference to a recent conversation of mine with **Andrew** , a boy of fifteen who phoned my office to seek advice on whether or not he was homosexual. Having never met him before, I asked Andrew if *he* thought he was homosexual. 'Yes', he said, he did. I asked why. 'Because', he answered, 'one of my mates says I look like a "bird".' The logic of the remaining part of our conversation goes something like this: if you look like a woman, then you can't be a 'man'; you must, therefore, be a 'homosexual'.

On the basis of this and, I regret to say, countless other folk interpretations of sexual behaviour, I feel that to discuss the subject of homosexuality with any degree of clarity, we must first define our terms. This, of course, is easier said than done. Take, for example, the term 'homosexual'. The homosexual, some say, is one who engages in sexual activity with someone of his or her own sex. Nothing, it might appear, could be less controversial than that. Yet such a *behavioural* definition is woefully incomplete, for it says, in effect, that homosexuals only differ from heterosexuals in the use they make of their sexual organs.

If we pause for a moment to reflect on this definition, we soon realize its inadequacy. Emotions are, in the total make-up of gays, every bit as important as genital manipulation. If we are to accept a purely behavioural definition of homosexuality, then what is to become of those whose desires and preferences for their own sex are repressed or unfulfilled? Or those who engage in heterosexual activities without being, in any 'technical' sense, heterosexual? Or those who engage in homosexual activities without being, in any 'technical' sense, homosexual? How should we regard these people?

The point I wish to make here is that serious problems of definition do exist which can seriously hamper our understanding of those we wish to help. In its determination to isolate 'homosexual' and 'heterosexual' into mutually exclusive categories of sexual behaviour, society has oversimplified the infinite range of human sexuality and substituted a system of classification and labelling which takes little account of human variety. By way of proof, consider the following four stories told by Felix, nineteen; Alec, forty-six; Tom, forty-seven; and Gerald, twenty-four.

I first met **Felix** in late 1974 at a GLF disco in London, where he played saxophone in a rock group called The No Name. At present Felix spends most of his spare time studying, which means 'listening to Vivaldi and Bach and maybe, if I'm in the mood, to Mozart'. He plans, in the not too distant future, to resume his music studies, and hopes eventually to have saved enough money to go to New York and enrol at Juilliard. Though Felix's sensual experience has been with both sexes, he tends to make a firm distinction between emotional involvement, on the one hand, and 'sex for gratification, for the fun of it', on the other. 'I'm a sexual opportunist, I guess', he says, by way of explanation. Thus, although Felix has developed strong emotional feelings for both men and women, these have not generally led to sexual involvements. 'I just don't know what that would lead to, is why, and I don't see how, just now, I'd hassle through it if the other person couldn't let go. Still, who knows? I keep changing, so I can't say for certain if I'll always feel this way.' Does Felix regard himself as either gay or straight? 'I'd say I'm roughly two-thirds straight, *today*,' he replies, 'though tomorrow it could well be the other way around. Let's just say I'm *polysexual*.'

Unlike Felix, **Alec**, only fully recognized his homosexual component at the age of forty-two, nearly four years ago. It was then that he met Michel, a twenty-five-year-old schoolteacher from Paris who was, at the time, on holiday in London. 'I fell in love almost instantly', says Alec, 'and have never once questioned my feelings since the day we met.'
For the past three and a half years Alec and Michel have faithfully alternated in their monthly visits to London and Paris to see each other. They have made no plans to live together, as Alec is married and the father of five children ranging in age from six to twenty.
So far Alec, because of the nature of his business, has managed to explain his week-end absences to the satisfaction of his wife without, he hopes, arousing any suspicions. 'Though I don't know my luck will hold out for ever', he says, cautiously. And if his wife discovers? 'We'll cross that bridge when we come to it. This is all a "question-mark" in my mind. I would hope, if she were ever to discover, that she might try and understand that I love her and the children, but that I love Michel, too. This is the way I am. . . .' 'Perhaps having two loves seems selfish to you', says Alec; 'I know it does to most people. But during these past four years, I've been as loving and, really, rather more so, than ever before, and to *everyone* involved, including, of course, the children. I'm happier now, so I feel I have much more love to give . . .'

'What I long for, says **Tom**, 'is a loving and mutually pleasurable relationship. This isn't easy for me, since my sexual preference is for children under the age of twelve . . . both sexes.
'People, you see, don't accept the sexuality of children. They teach children to be distrustful of an older person's attentions. . . . This makes it very difficult. Call me what you like—heterosexual, paedophile, or both . . . no, not

homosexual. I'm not homosexual, though many have
thought so. . . .

'I was married at eighteen. My wife and I lived together for,
oh, some fifteen years, right up till she found out about me.
Then she left me. . . .

'I was always this way, though I couldn't accept it till
eight, nine years ago. . . . Paedophiles, you see, are still
moral lepers, and worse, in the eyes of the public; and "child-
raping monsters" in the eyes of the law.

'How many people realize that the average paedophile is as
much opposed to child-molesting as the average man in the
street? . . . Like I said, I look for a loving relationship. I love
children, and I want to be tender with them.

'You know, if people could open their minds, they'd find a
great deal that they don't know much about. And one thing
is paedophilia.'

Gerald is now twenty-four years old and works in a wine shop in
central London. Between the ages of twenty-one and twenty-two
he served several months in jail for refusing to pay his rates.

'In gaol I shared a cell with a bloke they all called Babes.
"Babes", because he looked like a baby, a baby girl. He was
eighteen, pretty, and had soft, blonde skin. A person like that
has to be careful in jail. . . .

'I'm gay, but Babes wasn't. But gay or straight doesn't matter
in jail if someone fancies you, providing he's a big enough
lad. But I wouldn't do anything like that to Babes. I liked
him. . . . No . . . more than that, I loved him. Every day was
different with Babes around, even in jail. That's how he made
me feel.

'But good things don't last in this world, do they? After a few
months together, with no sex between us, mind, I began to
hear rumours. You have to remember, a day in jail can be very
boring. The lads think a lot about sex, and talk a lot about sex.
Some of them began to talk about Babes and me, because I
think they were jealous. I could tell by the way they looked at
Babes. . . .

'One day, then, when no one was around, two louts claiming
to hate gingers waited for us in the showers and took turns

raping Babes, while a third geezer held me back, covering my mouth with his hand the whole time.

'I'll never forget that. It's not that this kind of thing didn't happen often enough, it does. But this time. . . .

'Of course, Babes knew about me from the first. It didn't matter, though. But after the rape, his attitude seemed to change. I don't know why. He didn't talk so much, and he ignored me a lot. A few weeks later he was outside . . . and I've never seen him since.'

Each of these four stories illustrates one of the principal difficulties involved in fixing sexual labels on to people: erotic feelings are not always rigidly focused on one or the other sex (Felix), nor any particular age group (Tom), though they may be repressed until comparatively later in life (Alec), and then surface in extreme circumstances under a guise of aggression which defends the individual from the threat which same-sex feelings of tenderness or desire might pose (the 'heterosexual' inmates in Gerald's story).

Concerning patterns of sexual behaviour, the voices heard in the preceding pages should warn us against assuming that all human beings fall neatly and co-operatively into two antithetical classes, 'heterosexual' and 'homosexual'. This is not so, as Dr Kinsey and his associates have pointed out:

> The heterosexuality or homosexuality of many individuals is not an all-or-none proposition. It is true that there are persons in the population whose histories are exclusively heterosexual, both in regard to their overt experience and in regard to their psychic reactions. And there are individuals in the population whose histories are exclusively homosexual, both in experience and in psychic reactions. But the record also shows that there is a considerable portion of the population whose members have combined, within their individual histories, both homosexual and heterosexual experience and/or psychic responses.

The division of the world into 'sheep and goats' is a great mistake, Kinsey concludes, for 'it is a fundamental of taxonomy that nature rarely deals with discrete categories; only the human mind invents categories and tries to force facts into separated pigeon-holes.'[2]

Only by realizing that the world is a continuum in each and every one of its aspects can counsellors understand the realities of sexual variation, as well as the difficulties and confusions of some within our sexual minorities. Social reactions to gays have obviously been based on the general belief that homosexuals are unique and, as such, need special consideration or 'treatment'. When it is recognized that homosexual response and/or activity is not fundamentally different from that had by a substantial portion of the total population (according to Kinsey, some thirty-two per cent),[3] then attitudes will begin to change. Such recognition could also be of great potential help to judges and social workers, officials in the Army, Navy, and Merchant Marine, administrators of penal and mental institutions, clergymen, police, parents, and others who may be unaware of the incidence figures and who thus persist in calling for the condemnation, isolation, or institutionalization of nearly one-third of the nation's population.

Sex and Gender

In this chapter my principal concern is with questions of identity and definition. And because the gay person's very existence constitutes a challenge to the way society defines and categorizes human sexuality and its roles, such questions must also be of paramount concern to the counsellor. For the counsellor's role is to help the troubled gay define the nature of his or her conflict with society and, by so doing, to accelerate the process of self-identification. This, as we have seen, is a goal often thwarted by the careless use of sexual labels. Another major problem in dealing with issues arising out of social attitudes to sexual minorities is the general confusion surrounding the terms 'sex' and 'gender'.

Sex is not simply determined by biology, as most people would appear to believe; it is also *socially defined*. This fact is perhaps nowhere better illustrated than in the case of the transvestite, who, more than most in our society, understands the various ways in which each of us is conditioned from birth by the conventional dichotomies of 'man' and 'woman'. **Carl** is a transvestite, aged fifty, who lectures in physics at a college for further education:

I was thirteen years old when I first began to take an interest in women's clothes. I can remember walking down Oxford Street looking at the windows, noticing the women's clothes—dresses, in particular, and shoes, lingerie. I adored fabrics, too: silk, satin, velvet, lace. I wanted to wear them close to me. . . .

In the beginning, there wasn't an *overwhelming* desire to wear the clothes, though. But in my early teens I developed a strong identification with women and, alongside that, a need to be accepted as one. Not all of the time, but on occasions. From then on, I felt tense whenever wearing men's clothes.

Still, it wasn't till I was seventeen years old that I actually dressed in women's clothes. One day, when I was all alone in the house, I decided to put on one of my sister's dresses. When the time actually came to do this, I was paralysed with fear thinking I'd be caught. But mixed in with those feelings was a sort of sexual glow. . . .

It's difficult to explain to someone who's never experienced the feeling. It was very rousing, although later in life it would lose this connotation, and then it became something more generalized. . . .

In the early days, after wearing women's clothes, I would feel convinced for a long time afterwards that everyone knew my secret. Because at this time I still believed that there was no one else in the world like me. My main concerns were loneliness, and this sense of being 'unique'. It wasn't until years later, in fact, that I actually heard the word 'transvestite' defined, and knew that there were others like me. . . .

I left home at the age of eighteen and took a job in London, where I knew I could cross-dress with less risk. Four years later, after completing my A-level work, I enrolled at a teachers training college, and today I'm a full-time lecturer in physics. . . .

All this time in London I would be dressing quite frequently as a woman, both in private and, less often, in public. When I was twenty-six, I married, and I still enjoy heterosexual relationships today.

What most people don't understand is that transvestites do *not* want sex-change operations. That's the transsexual. I know I'm male, but I also wish to preserve my female self, despite this outward 'proof' of my male-ness. But don't forget, I speak only for myself. No one can speak for *all* transvestites, any more than for *all* homosexuals, or *all* heterosexuals, or all whoever. . . .

We were saying before that one is always forced into apologizing for oneself. People expect you to do that when you're different. But I'm done with that now. There's nothing that I feel the need to apologize for. I am this way; I *enjoy being* this way; and I'm not hurting anyone. If other people don't like me, that's *their* problem.

You know, when the 'experts' speak of people like me as unhappy, they don't have a *clue*. . . . It does annoy me! They don't appreciate the risks we run in being ourselves. . . . Certainly, I'm worried about people 'finding out'. And the reason is *other people* . . . other people and their reactions to me.

Let's face it: I can be arrested at any time and be publicly exposed. The only time you can safely cross-dress is at masquerades. . . .

What transvestites need, to begin with, is to be able to establish contacts with other transvestites. People also need to understand transvestism in terms of gender identity. It's more than simply wearing women's clothes; it's also a question of identification.

People who fail to distinguish between gender and sexual object choice are often inclined to regard the transvestite as a homosexual. As Carl's story reveals, this is often an incorrect assumption. In fact, according to a study involving 504 cross-dressers undertaken by a leading writer on the subject, Charles Virginia Prince, himself a transvestite, the majority of cross-dressers are heterosexual.[4] According to Prince, 'love of the feminine' is what characterizes the transvestite, and from this springs the desire to cross-dress. Yet not every cross-dresser is a transvestite, Prince insists: 'He may be a transsexual, a homosexual, a bank robber, or a person at a Hallowe'en party.' Here, as elsewhere, it's a taxonomic problem: 'Our society makes heterosexuality and homosexuality its chief distinction,' Prince argues, 'but you can cross-dress if you're either.'[5]

Transsexuals are often mistaken by the lay person as

transvestites due to the interest of both these sexual minorities in cross-dressing. Generally speaking, though, the latter group derives emotional, psychological, and erotic gratification from dressing in the clothes of the opposite sex, while the former views clothing entirely as a bodily expression of an inner identification. In other words, a transsexual is a person assigned by the anatomical structure of the body to one sex, but who feels to be, and wishes to function as, a member of the opposite sex.

Iona, who is twenty-nine, was referred in 1974 to the gender identity clinic (London) for sex-change surgery:

Biologically speaking, I'm a 'normal' male, that is I have the physical organs of a man. But inside I'm a woman. And I need to *live* as a woman. My problem is my body . . . it doesn't yet match the real me.

It's no good asking me to give psychological reasons to explain why I am as I am, because I don't care. For several years I listened to people telling me how I over-identified with my mother, how my mother was 'too loving', over-protective, and all the other put-downs. Now I say, 'Maybe so, but I'm no longer interested. It doesn't matter. This is *me*. . . .'

The difference between me and, say, a homosexual, is that the homosexual *knows* he's a man. He thinks to himself, I'm a man, and I also want to have sex with other men. Transsexuals, on the other hand, are *not* homosexuals. I do *not* want to have sex with someone who doesn't see me as a woman. It's as simple as that.

A lot of people are uncomfortable with me. They wouldn't want to be seen in the street with me. This reflects more *their* insecurities. They're worried that people may 'get the wrong idea' about *them*.

Other people react a little differently. They feel uncomfortable because they're not 100 per cent certain which sex I am. People, you know, will behave differently depending on which sex you 'belong' to. With me, they don't know. I'm disorientating. . . .

I'm pre-surgery, so I think about being a woman twenty-four hours a day. What else is there? I only want to be accepted as the person I know myself to be. . . . Once I'm accepted as a woman, well, we'll see. . . .'

According to Iona, most of her problems are not internal, but rather are imposed by others—from the reactions others have to her desire to be a woman. Instead of regarding her feelings as real and valid, society tends to accept Iona's transsexualism as a manifestation of a psychological disorder. In other words, society refuses to accept her definitions (thus making it difficult for her to be totally self-accepting) and characterizes her situation as a symptom of mental illness. Rather than doing as Iona does and accepting her gender feelings as they are, the 'experts' speculate on causes, thus rendering her opinions less valid than their own. Having made this point about definitions, let us return to the term 'homosexual', which we earlier attempted to define. In an ideal world, of course, no definition would be required; we would recognize, with Dr Kinsey, that there exists a continuum between homo- and hetero-sexuality, and that sexual behaviour reflects this continuity. This is not, however, an ideal world, and some workable definition must be found.

I am therefore using the terms 'homosexual' and 'gay', in a behavioural sense, to indicate any male or female with more homosexual than heterosexual experience in adult life; and, in a psychological sense, any male or female who is emotionally partial or erotically attracted to the same sex and who may or may not engage in overt relations with them. Thus, 'being homosexual' can refer to activity, preference, inclination, role, self-concept, status, or any combination of these; for example, a person who engages in homosexual activities but rejects the self-concept, or a married person who has the inclination but does not act on it.

How Are Sexual Preferences Acquired?

Before moving on to explore the ways in which gays recognize and learn to deal with their homosexual difference, we need first to consider the process by which human sexual preferences are determined. Contemporary science recognizes that all human sexual patterns are a product of learning and conditioning.[6] Human beings possess an inherent physiological capacity to respond to any sufficient stimulus, be it autoerotic, heterosexual, or homosexual. The tastes and preferences, goals and motives that determine any individual's pattern of sexual behaviour are *acquired* in the context of his or her unique experiences. It is, therefore, *experience* which determines the pattern of sexual responsiveness that becomes characteristic of a person.[7]

Prior to the development of experimental psychology it was generally assumed that human sexual behaviour depended upon innate, unlearned tendencies that were unrelated to an individual's environmental experiences. These instinctual influences were interpreted in terms of procreation, which was thought to be an inherent aim of the sexual drive. This is a view which, as we shall see in Chapter 5, is reflective of moral and religious, rather than scientific, concepts. Homosexuality and other 'non-procreative' manifestations of the sexual drive were therefore dismissed as statistically rare 'perversions' having little relevance to prevailing views of sexuality. This position is no longer tenable, however, as the data of Kinsey and others have clarified the importance of homosexuality in the lives of substantial numbers of men and women in all cultures and throughout all of history.

It is the inherent physiological capacity of human beings to respond to *any* sufficient stimuli that provides us with the basic explanation as to why individuals acquire their sexual preferences. There is no need to hypothesize biological factors (genes, chromosomes, hormones), fixation theories, theories of childhood parental attachments, interpretations of psychopathic behaviour, or whatever, to explain the acquirement of homosexual preferences. Not only are such theories unsupported by scientific research and biased by religious and moral assumptions, but they fail to take account of recent data which persuasively indicate that (using Kinsey's formulation) the factors leading to homosexual behaviour are:[8]

1. the basic physiological capacity of every mammal to respond to any sufficient stimulus;
2. the accident which leads an individual into his or her first sexual experience with a person of the same sex;
3. the conditioning effects of such experience; and
4. the indirect but powerful conditioning which the opinions

of other persons and the social codes may have on an individual's decision to accept or reject this type of sexual contact.

Though it is not possible to know precisely which experiences, or combination of experiences, may affect one's erotic orientation, childhood experiences have generally been emphasized. Advocates of cultural 'imprinting' claim that the age must be fixed at a period which coincides with the development of language, i.e. from eighteen to twenty-four months of age. Others, including the Freudians, claim that the Oedipal period of from four to six years of age sets the basic sexuality of a person, in addition to the all-important facets of the personality. Behaviourists, for their part, argue that the ages of six and seven are more likely terminal points in the determination of a person's sexuality.

While there is no question of the crucial significance of these early years, the importance of later years has been largely underestimated. Individuals do, in fact, show a great deal of fluidity in their sexual preferences well into adult life, when the acquisition of new tastes remains a possibility. In my own personal counselling experience, I know of many people who did not 'come out' until they first had years of heterosexual experience, been married, and raised children. Then, during their forties and fifties, they developed conscious homosexual desires. Why this is so is a question explored at greater depth in Chapter 6.

On Discovering One's 'Difference'

Society goes to great lengths to ensure that its values and standards are learned by the child and adolescent. Thanks to the efforts of such efficient socializing agents as the family, school, religious institutions, the media, peer groups, etc., it is hardly any wonder that the majority of youngsters are drawn to the opposite sex. This is even more understandable when one remembers that homosexuality is never presented as a viable alternative lifestyle, but only as a *problem* within the community. It is this basic lack of acceptance which prevents gays from understanding the true nature of their sexual preferences in the same way as heterosexuals do. In fact, the discovery of homosexual difference is often accompanied by intense confusion and anxiety, as in the case of **Jack**:

At about the age of eleven or twelve I began to feel attracted to some of the other boys in my class. I would want to be with them, and do things with them—kiss them, or see them naked.

I had a crush on one slightly older boy. He joined our class at the end of the term, right before the school holidays. I remember that I couldn't wait for September to come so that I'd be able to see him again, and maybe to sit next to him.

I was terrified by these feelings. I had never met or heard of anyone else who had felt like this. . . . I was really frightened, all the more because I felt so alone. There was no person I would dare tell. . . .

And I felt guilty, too. I regarded my thoughts as 'mucky' and 'sinful'. I couldn't tell my parents, either. I knew that they would be upset and hurt; or angry, even.

When these feelings later intensified, I would go to the library in the hope that somewhere in all those books I'd find someone like myself. I would read about boys who were lonely, unpopular, sensitive, misunderstood; about boys who hated sports and were ridiculed by their mates. But nowhere in all those books did I find anyone like *me*!

It wasn't until several years later that I associated 'being different' with 'being homosexual'. And it was at least another four or five years before I dared allow myself to think that the word 'homosexual' might in any way apply to *me*.

With all the best intentions in the world, many a counsellor in the past has told someone like Jack that he's 'only going through a phase' and that, in the goodness of time, he will 'grow out of it'. Many youngsters accept this advice only to discover, much later, that their feelings have strengthened rather than abated. Such a discovery often leads to even greater anxiety, as well as a loss of faith in those whom one traditionally relies upon in times of need.

The following excerpts from interviews illustrate some of the principal themes that appear time and again in stories dealing with the gay person's discovery of being different. To begin with, there is the sense of social isolation, of 'not belonging', as **Simon** and **Dora** describe:

> Before I even realized that I was gay, I felt different. It was a sense of not belonging, of being excluded by some understanding of classmates and friends that I was separate from the rest. I had no idea why this was. Later, I thought it had something to do with my shyness, a certain sensitivity, perhaps, and a generally non-aggressive manner (Simon).

> I felt alone, and different—as different as a circle in a world of squares. I didn't fit in *anywhere*, and I didn't believe anyone could be of help. There seemed to be a conspiracy of silence about the kind of feelings I had. I thought these feelings would go away if I ignored them—if I kept them secret in myself. But by doing this I found they soon became the most important part of me (Dora).

Another major theme that the counsellor will encounter is the feeling of 'being unique'. Both **Geraldine** and **Eleanor** experienced this.

> At about the age of thirteen I began to develop a crush on one of the other girls in my form. We'd sit next to each other, and meet after class. Quite often we would go to the Heath where we had 'our' bench. It was situated in a very secluded area. We would kiss, and even touch each other. At the time, though I enjoyed this, I felt it was wrong, even sinful. This was not only because it had to do with sex, but because I had never met another couple like us. We seemed totally unique, and that *had* to be wrong! (Geraldine)
> When I was growing up I always felt this vague feeling of discontent. It seemed to me that I had failed. My failure was in not being able to live up to some undefined but universally accepted ideal. In this I seemed unique—which is a very painful thing to be at that age. At times I felt so confused and frustrated by my feelings and emotions that I could scarcely endure it. I knew I was different from the other girls. About this there seemed no doubt in my mind, and certainly not in *theirs*. In that kind of situation, I can assure you, 'being different' means 'being worse' (Eleanor).

A further theme in stories dealing with the discovery of one's
difference is self-denial as a means of earning the acceptance of
one's peers. **Daphne** explains:

> All the girls were interested in boys. Of course! And being the
> good little joiner that I was, I entered into the spirit of things:
> I dated boys. I was about thirteen years old when I tried to
> take an interest in a dreadful boy called Joey, who knew I was
> interested in films. For him, films meant cuddling in the back
> row of the local cinema. I thought, well, I'll try; we'll see how
> it goes. And I did for several months, too, until I had
> established myself as 'all right' with the other girls.
> Unbeknownst to them, however, I was less 'all right' than
> ever. The reason is, I had at last defined my 'difference': it was
> that boys meant absolutely *nothing* to me!

And **Barry**:

> Other boys would never let me forget that I was different from
> them. They always called me 'cissy' because I wasn't 'hard'; I
> wore glasses; I played the piano; I was thin as a toothpick. All
> these things qualified me as a first-class cissy. But it wasn't too
> long before the word 'cissy' gave way to the word 'poof' and,
> in time, to even less pleasant terms. Because of these attitudes,
> and also because of my ignorance about sex, I denied my
> homosexuality till I was nearly thirty. . . .
> I tried dating girls during this time. I even had a long
> relationship with one girl. It was disastrous. I became very
> anxious and confused. I simply could not relate these
> difficulties with my fantasies about other boys. And it seems
> the more I tried to change myself in ways acceptable to others,
> the more unhappy I became.
> You can't run away from being different—no matter how
> hard you try.

Can Sexual Preferences be Redirected?

Conventional patterns of sexual maturity are painfully
unsuitable to gays, as the above stories reveal. Because the
awareness of being different precedes the knowledge of being
homosexual, many gays grow up regarding themselves as
'failures'—an assessment based on their inability or refusal to
conform to certain realities defined by convention. In order to

strengthen a positive self-concept, counsellors should encourage such individuals to resist the rejecting attitudes of others by developing their own independent standards. What happens, though, if gays seek advice on changing their sexual orientation? How does the counsellor reply if a homosexual says: 'I can't go on the way I am. I want to be a heterosexual'? Is it, in fact, possible to change one's sexual orientation? The short answer to this question is 'no'. To suggest anything else by way of reply would be cruel and misguided. Although the counsellor will sympathize with those gays who encounter difficulties in withstanding social pressures, the fact of the matter is that such difficulties are *as nothing* when compared with those involved in attempting to 'convert' to heterosexuality. In short, it is simply not possible to expect that, by conforming to a heterosexual pattern, one can be made 'straight', any more than that, by conforming to a homosexual pattern, one can be made 'gay'.

There is a great deal of scientific evidence to support this claim. In fact, the majority of psychiatrists have experienced almost complete failure in their efforts to 'convert' gay patients to heterosexuality. Even in the extremely few and largely unconfirmed cases of 'success' that have been reported, we find no follow-up studies whatsoever on the sorts of adjustments achieved by the newly-made 'heterosexuals'. Indeed, an ever-growing number of psychologists argue quite persuasively that only very temporary change has been offered in these cases, and that such people were, to begin with, 'atypical' in so far as they demanded very radical changes in their lifestyle, in addition to possessing large amounts of time and money for the extensive psychotherapy or analysis required.

Self-acceptance, rather than submission to prejudice, is much the wisest course of 'treatment' for the counsellor to pursue. Troubled gays must be helped to resolve the guilt and conflict about their sexual preferences. In line with this advice, and by way of conclusion, consider the testimony of Dr George Weinberg, a psychotherapist who has written several outstanding essays on the issue of 'conversion':[9]

From what I have seen, the harm to the homosexual man or woman done by the person's trying to convert is multifold. Homosexuals should be warned. First of all, the venture is almost certain to fail, and you will lose time and money. But this is the least of it. In trying to convert, you will deepen your belief that you are one of nature's misfortunes. You will intensify your clinging to conventionality, enlarge your fear and guilt and regret. You will be voting in your own mind for the premise that people should all act and feel the same ways.

Summary

This chapter began with a statement concerning the importance to the counsellor of empathy in understanding and communicating with those who seek help. The capacity to participate in another person's feelings or ideas will greatly facilitate an understanding of what it means to be different-as-homosexual in our society.

The gay person's first awareness of being different is complicated both by society's failure to present homosexuality as a viable alternative lifestyle, and by a general tendency to label all individuals as either 'heterosexual' or 'homosexual'. But for many people erotic feelings are not rigidly focused on one or the other sex (**Felix**) nor on any particular age group (**Tom**). Erotic feelings may, in fact, be repressed until comparatively late in life (**Alec**), often surfacing in the context of extreme circumstances (see the case of **Gerald**).

A major problem in dealing with social minorities is the confusion surrounding the terms 'sex' and 'gender'. One fact in need of the emphasis is that in our culture sex is defined both biologically and socially (**Carl**; **Iona**). I therefore use the terms 'homosexual' and 'gay' in both a behavioural and a psychological sense to refer to activity, preference, inclination, role, self-concept, status, or any combination of these.

The unique experience of each person's life history determines the pattern of sexual responsiveness that becomes characteristic of that individual. However, indirect and powerful conditioning agents (the opinions of other persons and social codes regarding homosexual behaviour) often prevent an individual from recognizing or fully understanding his or her gay component. Thus, the discovery of homosexual difference is frequently accompanied by intense confusion and anxiety (**Jack**), causing those concerned to experience a sense of alienation from others in their environment (**Simon**; **Dora**), or to regard themselves as 'totally unique' (**Geraldine; Eleanor**). Although these reactions may lead to a temporary denial of one's gay difference (**Daphne; Barry**), an exclusive pattern of sexuality can never be permanently denied by 'conversion'. Though the counsellor will attempt to alleviate the social pressures that sometimes cause gays to think in terms of 'cure', self-acceptance rather than submission to prejudice is the only viable approach to these problems of identity.

3
Passing through Oppression

'No man, for any considerable period, can wear one face to himself, and another to the multitude, without finally getting bewildered as to which may be the true.'
—Nathaniel Hawthorne, *The Scarlet Letter*

This chapter will attempt to identify those social pressures which oppress gays and encourage a strategy of 'passing for straight', i.e. a double lifestyle: heterosexual on the outside, homosexual on the inside. But, first, let us consider the phenomenon of 'passing' as a means of avoiding oppression.

The Passing Phenomenon

The homosexual is a member of a social minority. Unlike other minority groups, however, gays can hide their distinguishing difference from the rest of the world. This crucial fact of the homosexual's existence explains why gay people have been so long in demanding their rights. In having to stand openly as a member of an oppressed minority, one develops a sense of group identification, a sense of sharing his or her own 'differentness' with others of one's own kind. Not so the homosexual, who is able to blend imperceptibly into the heterosexual mass without ever having to face the experience of standing openly with other gays as a member of a social minority. It is for this reason, more than any other, that many gays are less likely than other groups to understand their situation as social outsiders.[1]

Researchers are agreed that roughly three out of every four gays 'pass' as a means of avoiding social sanctions throughout most of their lives.[2] This high ratio is all the more disturbing when one considers that the figures include a disproportionately large number of individuals who are prepared to identify with gay groups and organizations.[3] To understand this seeming contradiction, it is necessary to look more carefully at the phenomenon of passing and assess its significance in the experience of gays.

Passing is generally defined in the metaphor of theatre, that is, playing a role: pretending to be something that one is not. In the context of homosexuality, however, the emphasis should be placed on *concealment* rather than *pretence*. Hence, to 'pass' is to camouflage one's gayness by withholding information about oneself that might lead others to identify one as homosexual. Such a strategy of passing, motivated as it is by anticipation of the negative sanctions that would follow discovery, inevitably leads to increased confusion about one's sexual feelings, as well as a heightened sense of guilt and shame.

This passing strategy is not confined to the self-rejecting homosexual, either. Even those who have come to appreciate their gayness as an integral component of their self-identity will not always be completely free of the need to live a double life. As **James**, twenty, wrote to me:

> Most of my friends know I'm gay. I've either told them, or they've worked it out for themselves. They're not naïve. . . . I'm always aware of my gayness. It's difficult not to be always 'aware'. It's a straight world, and you are always being reminded that you're different. . . .
> I'll be talking to people, not necessarily friends, but acquaintances, neighbours, the postman, the shopkeeper, and the conversation will turn to the subject of girls. I'm young, and they feel they can ask me these questions. They assume that, like themselves, and like everyone else in the world, I'm straight, and that I have straight interests.
> I listen to them and smile, in a friendly way, yet all the while hoping they'll move on to other subjects. I don't want to say, 'Sorry, you don't understand; I'm gay', because most people aren't prepared to hear that. They don't *want* to hear it, either. Most people don't have the imagination to transcend this assumption of theirs that everyone that *they* know is going to be straight.
> I know that this is not always such a big problem. And perhaps it is an educational experience for people to learn that someone they know is actually gay. But what about my feelings? It's difficult being 'that gay boy' all the time, having

to deal with the negative or shocked reactions of people when you tell them that you're gay or, even, of having to deal with people who know but who now see you *only* as a homosexual. I understand why people should think of me exclusively in terms of homosexuality. Perhaps I'm the only gay person they know (or *think* they know). But I get tired, sometimes, of having people look at me, however sympathetically, as a curiosity or an outsider. Worse yet, as someone to be pitied. And this is why, sometimes, I choose not to tell them I'm gay. I just keep quiet.

Being on stage, as gay, twenty-four hours a day is, as James implies, very demanding. It is difficult to be spontaneous in one's relations with people when one is seen always as a *type* rather than an *individual*. Yet such passing problems are minor compared with those confronting gays who *never* feel able to present themselves honestly to others, always being careful to manage their behaviour so as to maintain a pretence of heterosexuality.

Such concealment inevitably leads to alienation. The fear of exposure, of living a life that can be collapsed at any moment, forces one to be always 'on': to plot, to plan, to devise strategies of disguise and withdrawal. This anxiety follows closely on the heels of the decision to pass, as in the case of one seventeen-year-old girl, **Adele**, who was at last able to 'face up' to her gayness after months of worry, only to discover that

> . . . now, instead of having to worry about being a lesbian, I'm having to worry about anyone *finding out* that I'm a lesbian! I'm not certain I wasn't better off before. At least, before, I didn't feel such a hypocrite. Now I feel like an actress, always having to pretend I'm somebody I know I'm not. . . . I worry that people will see through me.
> Sometimes I think I'm not fooling anyone, least of all myself. I can never really tell whether people know or not. I'm always sort of looking after them to see if they have guessed.

Having to mask one's sexual orientation, like Adele, is not only conducive to anxiety; it can also create a permanent passing precedent. As author Robin Maugham writes in his autobiography, *Escape from the Shadows*, the decision to pass for straight—presenting 'a false façade to the world'—was the first step along the road to becoming 'two people'.[4] Such a schizophrenia of the human sensibility takes a heavy toll on the psychic state of the passer. Deceit of this kind quickly becomes a way of life, and the gay person emerges as one who is for ever alert to aspects of a social situation which others will treat as routine.

It is difficult to maintain one's self-respect under such circumstances, and the voluminous research of sociologists like Laud Humphreys provides persuasive evidence to suggest that self-hatred is much stronger among covert, passing homosexuals than it is among overt gays.[5] Thus, when **Gary**, a civil engineer in his late thirties, listened in affirmative silence to the 'queer joke' stories of his friends, it is hardly surprising that he should have come away convinced that

> I had degraded my character by offering tacit approval to the insulting stereotypes they drew. I listened to these stories of 'Larry Grayson gays' without saying a word. I even smiled, on occasion, which only appeared to confirm that I consented to everything they said.
> And yet, it was really *me* they were laughing at. Had I been braver, I would have said something. But I was afraid they would put two and two together and guess that I was gay, too. Then the mood would have changed in an instant, and I would have been the focus of attention. Only gays know what it feels like to be in that kind of situation. . . .
> I feel very ambivalent about effeminate gays. I'm not certain why. I hate the way they flout convention, mincing and fluttering about, drawing attention to themselves.
> Perhaps I don't mean that. I suppose it's no better or worse than the way straights behave, is it? I've been told that, really, I'm afraid of drawing attention to *myself*, to my homosexuality. Maybe so. But to be totally candid with you, I still avoid 'queens' at all costs; if you are seen with one of them, then that is it! Everybody knows about you!
> I don't like to hear myself say these things, but I can't help the way I feel. It takes time to change. It's easier to alter your behaviour than it is to change your psychology. . . .

One of the many negative effects of passing is the need of passers to take extreme measures in order to ingratiate themselves with unsuspecting heterosexual friends, e.g. by disassociating themselves from other gays or gay 'types'.[6] Thus, for Gary, 'Larry Grayson gays' were doubly disturbing: first, because they presented an unacceptable image of homosexuality to others (and, therefore, to himself); and, second, because their very existence enhanced the possibility of his own 'exposure' as gay ('they would put two and two together and guess that I was gay, too').

It is understandable that those who have internalized society's sex/role assumptions should make such strenuous efforts to prove, both to themselves and to others, that, despite appearances to the contrary, they are every bit as 'normal' as everyone else. Yet such a strategy of survival often produces intense feelings of anxiety and self-hatred. For this reason, passing for straight is the most efficient means available of destroying group cohesion among homosexuals; there is no better way than this to stir up mutual animosity and create a community of persons who think so little of each other and who offer one another so little comfort and love.

Passing as a Product of Oppression

The passing strategies outlined above may seem somewhat extreme. The majority of gays will not be so concerned with hiding or disguising their homosexuality. However, the issue is not the numbers of people who behave in such ways but, rather, the extent to which such alternatives to self-acceptance reflect the pressures that force some gays to regard them as inevitable. If, as Laud Humphreys maintains, the 'self-destructive ego is a product of oppression', then only the loosing of bonds will heal it.[7] It is my thesis that passing is largely motivated by an assumption of failure, a conviction that one has failed to measure up to society's concept of 'man' and 'woman'. As Dennis Altman has pointed out,[8] our society is one that defines masculinity and femininity very much in heterosexual terms, so that the social stereotype (and, often, self-image) of the gay is that of someone who rejects his or her masculinity or femininity. Those who are unwilling to accept their socially defined roles are appropriately stigmatized. Proving one's 'manhood', or being a 'lady', are thus closely tied up with the rejection of homosexual characteristics. In women, repression is often internalized; in men, it is often externalized in aggressive behaviour.

What is so fundamentally wrong and cruel about this ideology of sexual repression is that, in encouraging the adoption of rigid postures as a means of rejecting tender, warm, or loving feelings towards others of the same sex, society further inhibits many gays from exploring either the meaning or the value of same-sex closeness. Society does not wish homosexuals to form loving relationships: hence the difficulty for some of ever doing so. It's as simple as that. (This is a point further explored in Chapter 7.)

The mechanics of this socially induced repression are clearly described in three recent autobiographies by homosexuals. In the early chapters of *To Fall Like Lucifer*, the former MP Ian Harvey recalls that 'particular friendships', even those 'strong enough to be called love', were quite common in his student days. Yet a combination of secrecy and contempt always surrounded gay love, which was, he says, 'regarded as effeminate, and effeminacy in our eyes was degrading'.[9]

The experience of T. C. Worsley, the drama critic, further illustrates how stereotyped definitions of masculinity/femininity are transmitted and internalized. While a student at Marlborough, Worsley's yearning for acceptance led to a passion for games which, in turn, satisfied a need for reassurances about his virility. But friends of a more conventional frame of mind demanded additional proof, which took the form of the cricket captain's cousin—an attractive and 'experienced' girl who suffered silently through several physically uneventful sessions with Worsley before at last informing him:[10]

> 'You're a homosexual! . . .'
> 'Am I?' (Worsley replied, with genuine surprise).
> For how was I to tell? The word, after all, implied if anything, 'cissiness'. Cissy I certainly wasn't. Wasn't I, on the contrary, if not a tough, at least a very masculine, athlete?

But the most outstanding example of society's success in programming sex/role expectations is the case of William Aaron. Beauty for him was in the eye of the heterosexual, and it is there that he found himself to be ugly. 'Disgusted' by what he regarded as his homosexual 'retreat from normalcy', Aaron yearned to be 'reconditioned', 'a lover of women and therefore a complete man' (i.e. one who has 'penetrated a woman' sexually). As Aaron explains it:[11]

> I'd love to be able honestly to downgrade the importance of this 'achievement', to pose as someone so rational and 'together' that I could separate potency from masculinity; make a humane distinction between manhood and the ability to perform sexually with a woman. But that would be a lie.

The experience of William Aaron, like those of Ian Harvey and T. C. Worsley, helps us to understand just how painfully unsuitable to gays are heterosexual patterns of sexual maturity. Sadly, too, they illustrate the extent to which internalization of these attitudes and values makes the phenomenon of passing a key fact of the gay experience. Self-acceptance can be a reality only when gays are enabled to evolve a means of proudly embracing their sexual identity. Part of this adjustment involves an understanding of the means by which society stigmatizes homosexuality, and this we shall consider next.

Weapons of Oppression: The Law

No one who has ever counselled homosexuals can be in much doubt about the continuing reality of gay oppression under the law. For those who are not totally familiar with the subject, however, a brief introduction follows.[12]

Gay people in Britain encounter oppression of two basic kinds: persecution and discrimination. Persecution refers to the illegality of homosexual activity, and discrimination to its social and psychological consequences. So long as our society continues to legislate morality, it is fairly obvious that large numbers of people will consistently and consciously break the law. Not all these people will pay for their 'crimes', of course; in fact, it is quite safe to assume that only a small fraction will ever be apprehended. But those who do run foul of the law may well find their lives dramatically altered as a result; so, too, the lives of their friends and loved ones. Those who are not apprehended may be more fortunate in so far as they escape the wrath of the law; however, the awareness of one's lawlessness is bound to have damaging psychical consequences in the long run.

The Sexual Offences Act was passed by Parliament in 1967, ten years following the published Report of the Wolfenden Committee.[13] Regarded by many at the time as a piece of enlightened legislation, it has since been shown that in certain crucial respects the Act upholds and reinforces many of the traditional biases against male homosexuals. Although the Act legalized sexual activity between consenting males over the age of twenty-one, time has proved that certain provisions of the Bill are more harmful than beneficent in their effects:

1. members of the Armed Forces and Merchant Navy may not participate in homosexual activity, regardless of the circumstances in which such activity takes place;

2. homosexual acts between consenting adults in Scotland and Northern Ireland remain, in law, criminal offences;

3. homosexual males are not accorded the same latitude as heterosexual males in so far as the right to privacy is concerned, e.g. homosexual acts are illegal if performed on premises where more than two persons are present, even if they are all over the age of twenty-one, consenting, and in absolute privacy;

4. no provision is allowed for amendments to take account of changes made in other legislation, e.g. at present the age of consent for male heterosexuals is sixteen, but twenty-one for male homosexuals;

5. homosexual males are not accorded the same parity of treatment under the law as heterosexual males in respect to penalties, e.g. two years can be given for indecent assault on a woman, but ten years for indecent assault on a man;

6. no fair and just balance between the concepts of freedom and protection is achieved, e.g. in regard to cases of soliciting: police evidence is sufficient *in itself* (the complainant not being called upon to give evidence) to substantiate a charge made by one man against another; it is an offence for a man (or woman) to solicit another man for 'an immoral purpose', but not for a man to solicit a woman for an identical purpose;

7. the law assumes that male homosexuality is more antisocial than heterosexuality (and, therefore, inherently more criminal), e.g. by the use of such negatively toned words and phrases as '*lewd* homosexual practices' [emphasis added].

One final point: the 1967 Act, in line with all past legislation dealing with sexual morality, does not prohibit homosexual behaviour between women. In fact, when a private Member introduced a clause into a 1921 Commons Bill, it was rejected by the House of Lords on Government advice which argued that such a measure, in addition to encouraging blackmail, would involve unwarrantable interference with the freedom of the individual.[14]

As far as prosecutions for homosexual 'offences' are concerned, most of these fall into one of two categories: breaches of the age of consent and sexual activity in a public place. Approximately eighty-five per cent of all 'age of consent' cases involve adult males charged with offences against one or (in about half the cases) more than one boy between the ages of eight and fifteen. In most instances the accused will plead guilty to the charges and be given a prison sentence of from one to ten years. A smaller percentage of men are placed on probation, fined, or given suspended prison sentences. If the accused has offered money as an inducement, or is a teacher, a social worker, or a member of one of the caring professions generally, then imprisonment is more or less automatic.[15]

The above account of existing legislation and prosecutions for homosexual 'offences', though brief, should be sufficient to alert readers to the fact that, in situations involving the law's attitudes to homosexuality, it will not always be an easy matter to determine the point at which counselling leaves off and social services begin. This point is borne out in the case of **Reg**, twenty-seven, who is at present living and working in North London. Reg is 'fortunate' in so far as his involvement with a sixteen-year-old boy never came to the attention of the law. But when he first came to see me, nearly two years ago, he felt certain that arrest was imminent. As he recalls:

I fully expected to be hauled into the police station, put on trial, and then be sent to jail for corrupting the morals of a minor.

I'll start at the beginning, when I first met Tony. Actually, I had seen him dozens of times before we ever spoke. We lived on the same road, just a few houses apart. Tony had moved in with his family about three months before. . . .

It was Tony, by the way, who spoke first. He was always a bit flirtatious, I should say. Oh, I had already noticed him, of course. He could tell that I was . . . curious. I guess it showed in my eyes.

It was during our very first conversation that he mentioned the fact that his parents were spending most week-ends in Norwich with his gran, who was poorly. 'Why don't you keep me company? We've a colour telly', he says. . . .

Well, to keep a long story short, I dropped round to see him that week-end, and on several other occasions. I needn't tell you again all that happened. Let's just say he wasn't in the least bit shy. Mind you, I wasn't unwilling; but it wasn't *me* who corrupted him. At sixteen he was well and truly corrupted, believe me, for all that innocent look of his. . . .

People talk about predatory old men in dirty macs! It was *he* who seduced *me*! And as for being a dirty *old* man, I was barely twenty-five at the time. . . .

I'll skip to the point. Tony's parents discovered that the two of us had been seeing one another, and they threw a fit. Obviously Tony made it appear as if I had hypnotized him or something because they *really* were outraged. . . .

There was no doubt in my mind they were going to the police. In fact, I couldn't be certain they hadn't already done so when I came to see you. The father was *furious*!

But then you spoke to them, and I suppose that changed his mind. . . .

In fact, Tony's father had little inclination to discuss matters rationally when I first spoke to him over the phone. Tony's mother proved far more sympathetic to Reg's situation, as well as to her son's. It was she who arranged for a meeting of the two families, urging her husband 'not to take things so personally'. This advice was much to the point. Many fathers view their sons, at least in part, as proof of their own masculine accomplishments. For this reason their self-image is threatened should the son exhibit homosexual tendencies, or express feminine traits, or prefer artistic pursuits to games and sports. Tony's father was therefore perfectly prepared to believe, in the face of much evidence to the contrary, that his son had been seduced by Reg.

Some semblance of the truth did emerge, however, when the two families met to thrash the matter over, and Tony's father finally decided it would be best to 'keep this whole affair to ourselves'. It was not so much the 'truth' which persuaded him to take this course of action but, rather, the argument of Tony's mother that to file a complaint with the police would do their son far more harm than good. In this opinion the Wolfenden Committee appears to be in complete agreement: 'The fact of being seduced', it says in its Report, 'often does less harm to the victim than the publicity which attends the criminal proceedings against the offender.'[16]

As for Reg's parents, though shaken by the manner in which they learned of their son's homosexuality, their love and concern for Reg has in no way changed. As **Alice**, Reg's mother, says:

We had a long talk, and I'd say we understand each other a little better now. Mind, things won't ever be the same way as before. They can't be, really.

I'm having to look at my world differently. I've changed some of my ideas. The future looks a bit different. Reg is our only child, and I know I won't be a grandparent now. . . .

I can't say I'm in any way pleased Reg is homosexual. I'm sorry, but I can't. . . . My generation is one which looked at things very differently than what they do today. Like I said to Harold, I know it's old-fashioned, but it's the way I am. . . .

I'm trying to do the best I can. I can't do better than that. . . .

You see, this is all new to us, Harold and me. We've never had to think about . . . this, or anything like this, before. . . .

Still, Reg is our son, and we love him. . . . He's not changed, has he, just because we know? If anyone has changed, I suppose you can say it's us.

The reaction of parents to their children's homosexuality will be further considered in Chapter 6. For now, it is sufficient to say that the suffering caused by the five-year disparity in the age of consent is by no means limited to those taking part in homosexual activity. The families of those involved also suffer in consequence of a law which, as Bob Sturgess has argued:[17]

is a bad law . . . because it invites—and suffers—widespread violation by otherwise law-abiding citizens; bad because the ministering professions are also prone to disregard it in the name of common humanity; and bad, finally, because it is not in accord either with current knowledge or with this country's best traditions of toleration and enlightened reform.

Homosexual activity can also be prosecuted under the Sexual Offences Act of 1956, s. 32, which states: 'It is an offence for a man persistently to solicit or importune in a public place for immoral purposes.' Though originally intended to deal with men procuring for female prostitutes, it has, in practice, been directed almost exclusively against gay men in situations having nothing to do with prostitution, but which, rather, involve unobjectionable pick-ups and casual encounters.[18]

Unhappily, the police, despite the fact that they are no longer under any obligation to detect homosexual activity between consenting adults, continue on occasion to treat gays as if the very fact of their sexual orientation was an indication of anti-social tendencies. Indeed, recent cases known to the Albany Trust and the Sexual Law Reform Society indicate that patterns of arrest in public places, as well as interrogation procedures concerning aspects of a man's private life which are no longer criminal, give cause for continuing concern.[19]

Although the police insist that they no longer use *agent provocateur* tactics, the overwhelming evidence of many homosexuals contradicts this claim and, I am convinced, demands the most serious consideration by the counsellor. Let us listen to the voice of **Jeff**, whose story reveals many of the circumstances which frequently lead to the arrest of a gay person in a public lavatory.

I'm twenty-nine and I'm currently unemployed. Six months ago I was arrested for soliciting in a public gents. I pleaded guilty. The judge gave me a £25 fine.
At the station they told me that my employer would be informed, so I quit. I quit my job the next day. I didn't want to be fired first.
I won't deny that I've cottaged from time to time. But on the afternoon of my arrest, I wasn't looking for anything but a quick pee.
Why did I plead guilty, then? Ask anyone who's been in the

same spot, and they'll give you the same answer: because the police tell you it will go easier for you if you do. They act like they're concerned, like they're giving you this advice in your own interest.

And you want to believe it, you know, because, let's face it, you're scared, you're in a panic. So you go along with their story. You plead guilty. Later on, you appear in court. You pay your fine. It's over. A minimum of fuss. And you don't want fuss, because that's bad for you, for your family, friends, job. It was bad for *me*, and I pleaded guilty!

People don't believe you, either. They think, well, you know, the police, they don't lie. They're the police! You have to put your trust somewhere, don't you? People don't want to believe cops aren't perfect. So you must have done what they say you did.

The day I was arrested, I had gone into a toilet at 5.30 in the afternoon. Maybe a little later. It was crowded at that hour. The urinals were all taken up, so I started to leave. Then this bloke zipped up and left, and I went over to this urinal next to a skin-head type in faded denims.

I wasn't looking for 'action', but you'd have to have been blind not to have seen this bloke next to me playing with his penis, and looking right down at it, with a sort of frown on his face. I looked over at him, not obvious, though. Just a glance to the left with my eyes, if you see what I mean.

Funnily enough, I was beginning to feel a bit nervous. I guess I suspected something. I couldn't urinate, either. I never can if I'm feeling nervous like that. I looked up, then, at his face. Just curious, because I thought to myself, is this bloke 'rent', or what?

It was at that moment, as I looked at the bloke's face, that this other bloke who'd been standing at the wash-basin combing his hair, he came over and put his hand on my shoulder. And with that the fellow next to me quickly zips himself up and looks at his mate, then at me.

They were cops. I couldn't believe it, because they told me I was under arrest. Then they took me back to the station house.

The police are anxious that the public should understand that they do not enter toilets looking for homosexuals unless a complaint is lodged.[20] Let us assume that this is true. Who, then, makes the complaints? In the course of a sociological study involving close observation of hundreds of homosexual encounters in public rest-rooms, Laud Humphreys came to the conclusion[21]

> that an unwilling participant may withdraw at any time from a (cottage) encounter without creating a scene or losing his purity or his composure. Because of cautions built into the strategies of these encounters, no man need fear of being molested in such facilities; he must first demonstrate by showing an erection that he wants to get in on the action.

Humphreys is not alone in this conclusion. It is the carefully considered opinion of a research team on law enforcement at the University of California's Faculty of Law that[22]

> the majority of homosexual solicitations are made only if the other individual appears responsive and are ordinarily accomplished by quiet conversation and the use of gestures and signals having significance only to other homosexuals. Such unobtrusive solicitations do not involve an element of public outrage. The rare indiscriminate solicitations of the general public do not justify the commitment of police resources to suppress such behaviour.

One final provision of the law affecting gays to be considered here is the common law charge of conspiracy to corrupt public morals. This law is of immediate concern to the counsellor, for recent interpretations of the 1967 Sexual Offences Act aim to inhibit all those who recognize and are attempting to alleviate the social isolation and loneliness of gay people through the provision of social facilities and meeting places.

It was in June of 1972 that the House of Lords upheld convictions for conspiracy to corrupt public morals brought against the directors and company of an 'underground' newspaper, *International Times* (*IT*). The prosecution arose because *IT* published contact advertisements for gays who wished to meet with other gays. Despite the fact that the prosecution never suggested the homosexual meetings or activities envisaged by the ads were in any way unlawful, the court ruled that there is a 'material difference' between 'exempting certain conduct from criminal penalties' and 'making it lawful in the full sense'.[23] In other words, the Sexual Offences Act of 1967 was read as saying that if people chose to corrupt themselves (i.e. if homosexuals chose to meet and engage in sexual activity) they were entitled to do so, and the law would not interfere. On the other hand, no licence had been given to others (e.g. counsellors?) to encourage such a practice of 'corruption'.

It seems, as one lawyer writing in *The Guardian* has recently pointed out, that we are, in regard to homosexual behaviour, in a no-law area where 'the law now appears to be what the Director of Public Prosecutions wakes up in the morning and says it is'.[24] As a consequence, police are given wide powers of discretion in carrying out their duty to preserve the peace and protect the 'public good'. Thus, police can and do infringe upon the civil rights of gays who are not conducting themselves like heterosexuals. Consider this story, reprinted from *New Society*:[25]

In September 1968, the Manchester magistrates fined a club owner for having allowed men to dance together. Evidence was given by the police who had visited the place in plain clothes that it was 'a haunt of homosexuals'. Presumably the homosexuals themselves were not outraged by single-sex dancing. Nevertheless, the owner pleaded guilty to having permitted dancing of a nature likely to cause a breach of the peace.

Weapons of Oppression: Employment

It is not only the law that oppresses homosexuals and encourages passing. Discrimination comes in a great variety of shades, as **Eileen**, thirty, explains:

Rejection is expressed in many ways. The law in this country has never discriminated against women *as lesbians*, yet I don't feel any less oppressed than gay men.

The hushed conversations people have about 'one of them'; the newspaper stories about lesbian scandals that are blown out of all proportion; the jokes about 'dykes' and 'bull dykes'; the sexist assumption that 'all we need' to be 'real' women is a

'good man' (and you-know-what-else!); the icy stares that
greet you when you arrive at dinner parties with a girl friend
rather than the expected boy friend; the social functions you
never get invited to because you 'simply don't fit in'.
I could go on endlessly, relating my experiences and those of
my friends. I won't, though, because you're always thought
'paranoid' when you say anything. One is always thought
paranoid by people who have no idea what it's like to be
someone else.

Nowhere is discrimination more pronounced than in the area of
jobs and employment. The counsellor will doubtless encounter
many cases where, in being open about themselves at work,
homosexuals have jeopardized their prospects for promotion,
or even lost their jobs (though other reasons are generally
given in such cases). The risks run by self-respecting gays is, of
course, peculiar to their status in society; hence, doing one's job
well is not always sufficient in itself to prevent the gay person
from being sacked. Professions particularly at risk are (in
addition to the military) those in government, the church,
education, the social services, and caring professions; elsewhere
efforts are frequently made to keep 'known homosexuals' out of
'sensitive' posts.

It is sometimes thought that gay women, because of their
more favourable legal status, encounter less discrimination than
men in this area of employment. This is not so, and counsellors
will eventually find themselves confronted with women from all
spheres of work who seek help with broken careers. For **Nancy**, a
twenty-eight-year-old former nurse, the problem was one of
'not knowing for sure whether anyone knew, or whether, really,
it would make a difference if they did':

There are a lot of gay nurses. It's an open secret. But don't
mention the subject to *other* nurses. They take the attitude that
it gives the profession a 'bad name'. It's the wrong image to
present to the world outside. . . .
I remember once confiding in an older nurse while in
training. She was straight. I felt so lonely then. I told her
about myself because I was looking for understanding. I was
very young. Her immediate reaction was to assure me
repeatedly that I shouldn't breathe a word to anyone else. She

left me feeling that mine had been an unwelcome confidence. After that, we scarcely talked when we passed in the wards, except to nod, or say 'hello'.
I felt frightened by this reaction. 'Discovery' suddenly loomed as an awful possibility in my life. I would have to keep up my guard, pretend to be straight. This is how I interpreted her reaction. . . .
In many ways it's fortunate that I didn't come out until recently. I don't believe I could have lasted those five years in hospital otherwise. Even so, it was difficult sticking it for that long. . . .
Being a nurse . . . I don't know . . . it's not easy separating the profession from the rest of your life. You have to be open about yourself, otherwise you always find yourself in difficult situations, always pretending. . . . It's the small talk, for example, with all the girls enthusing about 'the kidney case' in such-and-such a ward, or 'Dr Mallory's latest patient', or whatever. . . .

It's having to *pretend* all the time! Using the body language women are expected to use in conducting business with male colleagues and patients! I had become my own worst enemy, pretending to be something that I wasn't, because that's what other people wanted.
It wasn't till I started talking to other *gay people* that I began to realize what was happening to me, and what I could *be*. . . .

Nancy's story helps to explain why so many homosexuals fear coming out, preferring instead to hide or disguise those facts about themselves which might lead others to the right conclusions about their homosexual orientation.

Dennis Altman does not exaggerate, then, when he claims that[26]

. . . if I am simply *known* as a homosexual, I will encounter discrimination even at times when no one seriously believes my sex life is directly involved. This is most obvious in the field of employment, and there are homophile leaders who believe that *job discrimination* is the greatest single reason why homosexuals fear disclosure.
Outside certain areas of work, of which entertainment and some personal services are the major examples, one's career

can only be adversely affected if one is known as—or
suspected of being—a homosexual. . . .
In my (own) case I realized some years ago that I was
precluded from entering conventional politics, because I was
not prepared sufficiently to hide my homosexuality. There
are, of course, a number of politicians who are in fact
'closeted' homosexuals, but I would not be prepared to live
the quite tortured life of secrecy such men must suffer.

Organizations which work for homosexuals—both self-help
and referral agencies—report numerous instances in which
individuals, both men and women, have lost their jobs or have
been asked to vacate their lodgings because it was either known
or suspected that they were homosexual. And such allegations
are almost always made *without* any sexual misconduct being
alleged. As for those gay people who take recourse in the law,
they soon discover that a homosexual charge which is made in
court—no matter how trivial it may be—is usually followed by
the most disastrous professional (not to mention personal)
consequences. This is a point I have made elsewhere in this
chapter, but it is an important one which cannot be emphasized
enough.

Most liberal opinion in Britain is appalled by the persecution
and discrimination of gay people which I have outlined; and, no
doubt, it would support the efforts of groups such as the
Campaign for Homosexual Equality (CHE), the Scottish
Minorities Group (SMG), and the Union for Sexual Freedoms in
Ireland (USFI) in their drive to reform the laws affecting
homosexuals. Unfortunately, though, such toleration is not
incompatible with a suspicious and even hostile attitude
towards homosexuality—particularly when this psychosexual
orientation is perceived as posing a threat to such institutions as
(heterosexual) marriage and the nuclear family.

Tolerance must be replaced by both understanding and, most
of all, by acceptance of homosexuality as a valid lifestyle. Until
such time as attitudes are substantively changed, however, gay
people will continue to regard passing as an attractive
alternative to being open and self-accepting. And such a
decision, as we have seen, can only be accompanied by the most
unhappy consequences.

Summary

This chapter has been concerned with the phenomenon of 'passing' and the nature of that oppression which sustains it.

Passing means concealing information about oneself which might bring others to conclude that one is homosexual. This strategy of survival in a hostile environment inhibits spontaneity (**James**), and often leads to intense feelings of anxiety (**Adele**) and a sense of alienation (**Gary**).

Passing is the product of oppression, and we have examined here some present legislation which discriminates against the homosexual. As far as prosecutions for homosexual offences are concerned, most of these fall into one of two categories: breaches of the age of consent (**Reg**; **Alice**), and sexual activity within a public place (**Jeff**).

Discrimination comes in many shades, and it is not only the law that oppresses gays and inhibits the search for self-identity. For example, gay women, though they are not discriminated against as lesbians under present legislation, nevertheless feel the impact of anti-gay attitudes (**Eileen**), and are particularly vulnerable in view of the unwelcoming posture taken by certain professions, such as nursing (**Nancy**). It is only when such rejecting attitudes as these are substantively changed that gays will more fully accept themselves and reject passing as an alternative to being open.

4

The Halo of Marriage

'To be or not to be: that is the question.'—
Shakespeare, *Hamlet*, III.i.56

Hamlet's question of whether 'to be or not to be' is one with special resonance for homosexuals. Gay people, as we observed in the previous chapter, are confronted with a wide range of possibilities in dealing with the stigma attached to their sexual orientation. Almost as soon as gays have discovered their difference, the question arises as to whether or not they will reveal this fact to others. Many choose to pass for straight. Another form of adjustment, and one which is frequently overlooked in the literature dealing with the subject, is heterosexual marriage.

In this chapter, I shall consider the situation of married gays and the reasons why homosexuals enter into heterosexual marriage. Some modes of adjusting to the conflicts which develop in married life will also be considered. But first of all a warning regarding the statistical generalizations often made concerning the prevalence of marriage among homosexuals. Such figures must be viewed (as should so much else that has been written on the subject of homosexuality) with a fair degree of scepticism. The reason for this is that, generally speaking, only self-accepting and publicly identified homosexuals are interviewed by researchers, whereas the majority of married gays are likely to remain reticent about their homosexual component. This fact is not often taken into account, thus casting doubt on the accuracy of the present data.

The experience of many gay counsellors is that the number of gays who are, or who have been, married is higher than is generally supposed. Perhaps the following tentative findings based on my own counselling experience combined with the most recent and reliable statistical evidence[1] will be of some help

to readers in gauging the numbers of married homosexuals, the
ages at which gays are married, the duration of marriages, and
the numbers of gay parents:*

1. approximately one-fifth of all gays are married at some
   point or other in their lives;
2. approximately four-fifths of this number are married by
   the age of about twenty-nine, and the remaining one-fifth
   at a later age;
3. approximately three-fifths of all marriages among gays
   last for up to three years, and approximately two-fifths last
   for a period of more than three years;
4. approximately two-fifths of all married gays have had one
   or more children in the course of their marriages.

Why Gays Marry

Why should some homosexuals choose to enter into such a
seemingly conflicting situation as heterosexual marriage? The
reasons are various, but four explanations tend to be given with
greater frequency than others:

1. insufficient awareness of one's homosexuality at the time
   of marriage;
2. a conscious desire to escape in some degree from the
   knowledge of one's homosexuality;
3. rational choice;
4. social pressures.

Let us consider each of these in turn.

The story of **Judith** clearly illustrates the 'delayed recognition'
factor in the gay person's decision to marry:

> I didn't fully believe myself to be lesbian until some while
> after my marriage. I expect the evidence was plain enough for
> *anyone else* to see, but not me.

* Although it would be difficult to verify this conclusion, it is my feeling that
since the advent of Gay Liberation in 1969 fewer homosexuals choose to enter
into heterosexual marriages. My basis for this assertion is, in addition to my
own counselling experience, an interpolation of past and present research into
the incidence of marriage among homosexuals, e.g. Kinsey, *Sexual Behavior in
the Human Male* and *Sexual Behavior in the Human Female* (1948 and 1952);
Weinberg and Williams, *Male Homosexuals* (1974); and Saghir and Robins, *Male
and Female Homosexuality* (1974).

My first romantic crush was on a woman in her late thirties. I was about eleven or twelve. Very vaguely, too, I recall having had several dreams in which I was sexually involved with other girls at school. That's when I was about thirteen or fourteen.

But I never applied labels to myself. I mean, I never said, 'Aha! I'm lesbian!' *That* possibility never entered into my head. I wasn't aware homosexuality even existed.

In any case, I rather liked boys. More as companions, I think . . . as equals. Frankly, I felt superior to most boys I knew, though I enjoyed the company of the more intellectual ones. I'm afraid I was never much good at taking a subordinate or *submissive* role. . . .

Still, I dated. And there were one or two boys I was rather serious about. One boy, I discovered, was gay. He was nice—very sweet, intelligent, gentle, considerate. . . . We're still friends.

When I was twenty, I married Carl. Eleven months later I was pregnant. In the middle of my pregnancy Carl began to spend more and more time with his friends, or his hobbies. He had a number of outside interests. He was, and is, very interested in politics. So there's always been quite a bit to keep him away from home.

After Tim was born, I felt fairly content. Perhaps I should be ashamed of saying this, but I regarded being a mother as a challenge. I've always enjoyed taking on challenges. . . .

I certainly enjoyed those first few months of being a mother. But then, about four months after Tim was born, I was pregnant again. This second pregnancy was unexpected. I had been careless about taking the pill, and was beginning to feel very nervous about just everything. I was now seeing less of Carl, and although we never had serious arguments, it seems as though a formality had developed between us. . . .

After Mandy was born, I virtually refused to have sex. I don't think this greatly worried Carl. His lack of concern might have bothered me (on some level) if I hadn't been so pleased by his casual acceptance of the situation.

About a year later I met Mary, a girl I knew at my college some years before. She was sitting in the park, where I usually went in the afternoons with the children. . . . I saw her several days

a week after that. Within a few months we were in love. . . .
When I met Mary, everything changed. I began to see myself
more clearly. Three years after marriage I suddenly
understood: 'I'm gay!' I still like men, but it's basically
women I care for. . . . As I say, I don't know why it took me so
long to understand, and I don't care. . . .
I'm still married to Carl and, on the surface, at least, things
appear much as before I met Mary. But *I'm* changed. I'm
happier. I feel more complete.
Carl is away a great deal, but this is temporary. He begins a
new job in the spring. I can't say yet what will
happen—tomorrow or next year. One thing I can say,
though: I'm at last beginning to enjoy life.

Although Judith was unaware of her gay component at the time
of her marriage, it is probably true to say that most gays who
decide to marry are fully aware of their homosexuality. Some of
these decide on marriage as a means of escape: a 'solution' to
the 'problem' of being gay. Unfortunately, such an adjustment
is sometimes encouraged by counsellors in the belief that
homosexuality is a kind of situational phenomenon that will
disappear once the opportunities to have regular heterosexual
relationships present themselves. Consider, for example, the
case of **Toby**:

When I was seventeen I sought the advice of my doctor. I was
having these sexual fantasies about other boys. I thought
there might be something biologically wrong with me. . . .
My doctor's face turned crimson when I told him. He asked
me if I had told my parents. I said that I hadn't. 'Well, don't,'
he said, 'because many boys go through this sort of thing and
it doesn't mean anything.' No use worrying my parents, he
said.
He seemed more concerned about my parents than me. Yet I
did feel a *bit* better for having seen him. I hadn't realized that
other boys felt this way, too.
The trouble is, my fantasies continued. A few months later I
felt so depressed I went to a teacher. He became very solemn
when I told him. He asked me how long I had felt this way.
When I told him he seemed . . . well, I don't know, disturbed.

'Don't you have *any* feelings for girls?' he asked. But before I could answer, he was telling me how sensitive I was. He thought I was worried about taking advantage of girls, and that this concern had driven me to boys.

I didn't understand this. He seemed very encouraging, though, and told me I should think of marriage—having a family, children, responsibilities. He said that if I began going out more often with girls, I would soon find them less frightening.

I hadn't said anything about being *afraid* of girls. I *wasn't* afraid of girls. . . .

For the next year or so I forced myself to fantasize about girls whenever I masturbated. . . . At nineteen, almost on the spur of the moment, I asked this girl I had known for years to marry me, and she said 'yes', she would.

I truly believed that getting into the routine of marriage—having sex on a regular basis—would tone down my homosexual fantasies, make them less intense, less threatening.

It didn't work out that way at all. My fantasies were no less intense. Marriage was going to 'cure' me, but it didn't. After about a year, Millie and I almost began to hate each other.

Prior to his marriage, Toby had no sexual experience of any kind. This fact left him particularly susceptible to the advice of counsellors whom he believed to be experienced in this area. Other gays who marry are aware of their homosexuality as a permanent feature of their total make-up. Such individuals, under no illusions about the power of marriage to redirect their erotic preferences into heterosexual channels, still conclude that happiness is possible only by marrying and living out a conventional (heterosexual) home life. **Arthur**, thirty-five, is a case in point

I've always preferred sex with men. I never tried to deny that to myself. But by the age of twenty-nine I had given up believing in gay relationships. Basically, I was *afraid* to believe. . . .

I accepted, uncritically, everything people said about homosexuals. That made it easy for me to see only the

bitchiness, the broken affairs, the transiency. . . . And this I
didn't want for myself. I wanted something *permanent*. . . .
Right up to the time of marrying, I viewed my homosexuality
as a total negative. If that's the way you see yourself, then
everything in the gay scene is going to reinforce that
conviction, including gay partnerships.
I had this fantasy of a snug and secure family life. All my
friends, the people I grew up with, they were married, and . . .
yes, I envied them. I imagined family life as the ideal. You
know, you watch the box, you listen to the radio, you read the
papers, you talk with your friends, and it's always the family
that's assumed to be everyone's goal in life . . . the home,
family, getting married. . . .
For Margaret, my wife, marriage meant 'true love'. For me, it
meant security, being accepted as 'normal', being like
everybody else.

A fourth reason why some gays decide to marry relates to social
pressures. Being known about or being publicly identified as
homosexual may have undesirable consequences for those
concerned with maintaining a socially acceptable façade.
According to Erving Goffman, sex is more significant even than
social class, profession, or personal qualities in determining a
person's inner, as well as public, identity.[2] For **Edward**, a civil
servant, being married was 'a decided advantage' because '. . .
marriage imparted a respectable image':

> I'm not saying you must be married to 'get ahead'. But people
> do wonder when you're single after a certain age. And you
> must be above suspicion at all times. People are quick to jump
> to conclusions. . . .
> Certainly to be labelled 'homosexual' could lead to a variety
> of professional avenues being closed off. It can make a
> difference to one's career prospects . . . generally speaking,
> people don't require a great deal of evidence in order for this
> assumption (of homosexuality) to be made. . . .
> The insistent demands of one's relatives and friends who feel
> something is *wrong* with you, or in your life, if you've no
> marriage prospects—this constitutes a subtle form of
> blackmail. . . .
> It's assumed you're somehow irresponsible if you're

homosexual. Men who are married, family men firmly
ensconced in a conformist home life, are thought more
'solid'; marriage confers a halo of respectability upon them.

The demands of relatives and friends can be even more insistent
in the case of women. As **Cheryl** says:

> There are very strong cultural drives on women to be wives
> and mothers. Throughout childhood and adolescence I can
> remember hundreds of occasions at home when I was
> reminded of my future as some man's wife, or the mother of
> his children.
>
> At school, teachers never failed to emphasize the different
> roles and goals for men and women. The underlying
> assumption was that all women, except for the very
> unfortunate few, grew up, *matured*, and took their place
> alongside their men. Perhaps I was more conscious of this
> process of indoctrination because I always felt a man's lot was
> a more fulfilling one, potentially. . . .
>
> It's difficult to get free of the conformist cycle most of us are
> caught up in. I admire those women who do break out, but in
> those days I wasn't strong enough. You feel so desperately
> lonely and isolated when all your friends are dating boys and
> getting married. . . .
>
> I loved my parents and never wished to hurt them. It was from
> them that I learned what was expected of me as a daughter
> and a woman. I remember my mother describing 'poor
> Beryl', my cousin, as 'mischievous' and 'loose-moraled'. 'My
> poor sister,' she would say, 'the disgrace!' Mum would then
> compare me to Beryl, saying how happy she was that I never
> shamed her. I put the two messages together, and when I did
> they read: 'We love you, Cheryl, so long as you don't do
> anything *different* to disgrace us.'
>
> This is why, after becoming aware of my sexual feelings for
> other women, I understood that if ever I was to become a
> lesbian, I'd be unloved—as much an outcast at home as in the
> world outside.
>
> My parents, and especially Mum, were so worried I'd develop
> into a 'lonely old spinster'. How that term 'spinster' haunted
> me! Sitting by the fire, a little old lady with white hair,
> shoulders wrapped in a shawl. The thought of having no one

to look after me—no husband, children, grandchildren to keep me company. This frightened me. The day I was married, Mum says, was the happiest of her life. She's pleased I married Stewart, though, frankly, I think, in *my case*, it could have been 'most *anyone*. . . .

I know that Mum always sensed, deep inside, that I was different, but could never guess *how* I was different. She was very relieved, then, when I decided to marry. . . .

The Heterosexual Spouse

The above stories present the counsellor with a variety of motivation to account for the gay person's decision to marry: delayed recognition of one's true sexual orientation; conscious flight from the knowledge of one's homosexuality; rational choice; fear of loneliness; social and economic considerations; family pressures. But what are the reasons for the heterosexual partner's agreeing to marry a homosexual. The answer to this question is that, in most cases, the heterosexual spouse is not aware of his or her partner's homosexuality. This situation arises either because the gay person (e.g. **Judith**) is not conscious of being homosexual at the time of the marriage, or because the gay person chooses to keep this fact a secret (e.g. **Toby**; **Arthur**). However, if counsellors have the opportunity of meeting the spouses of gay people, they will also find that occasionally 'an undefinable difference' is what the heterosexual spouse regards as the gay partner's most attractive asset. This was so in the case of **Flo**, the young wife of Bruno:

I respected Bruno, and still do, for his gentleness and consideration. . . .
Bruno didn't tell me about being homosexual until quite recently. It must be the only thing he's ever kept from me. . . .
In a way I always knew. Oh, not that he was gay. I only thought he was different, but in a very special sort of way.

I suppose gay men don't try so hard to prove their virility. Most straight guys I've known make a big show at being manly. They have this hard exterior. I find it very difficult to relate to someone like that. You can't *talk* to them. . . .
Bruno always shared his feelings with me. This is something

else that made him seem so different. Most men feel it's cissy
to show their feelings.

. . . Unlike a lot of men, who are generally too proud to admit
they may be lonely, or in need of affection, Bruno was always
open and direct, never cold or distant.

There are also cases in which the heterosexual spouse takes the
decision to marry in the full knowledge that the partner is
homosexual. Some, like Meg, Vincent's wife, are 'too much in
love to let anything stand in the way'; others, like Perry, act in
the belief that the partner's sexual orientation 'will change after
being married for a time'; still others, like Evelyn, who are
relatively ignorant about homosexuality, are unable to accept
that this fact will 'in any way make a difference to the way we feel
about each other'.

Causes of Conflict

However optimistic the partners may be about the future of
their marriage, conflicts often do develop over waning sexual
attention and the formation of outside relationships. As
Vincent, Meg's husband, explains:

> I love Meg, in my own way. Not passionately. I respect her,
> though. My emotional involvement could never match her
> own for me. . . .
> Sexually, I've been . . . how does that expression go, 'I've
> been faithful to thee, Cynara, in my fashion'. . . .
> Meg tried to be understanding. She always meant well. But
> often her concern made me feel like an invalid. . . .
> There was quite a bit of sexual contact for the first six months
> or so. I enjoyed it. Of course, it didn't have the same meaning
> for me as I know it did for Meg. Still, I enjoyed it. Those who
> say that gay men are all frightened of women, or their bodies
> . . . they don't know what they're talking about.
> After about six months to a year, there was much less sex
> between us. I simply felt less inclined to express my feelings
> for Meg, sexually. Meg took this as an ominous sign. She
> thought she was losing me. She began to talk about having
> failed me. . . . The relationship grew very tense.
> It was then that Meg began to carp away about my being gay,
> about my gay friends. I told her, more out of anger than

anything else, that I was having an affair with Larry. She said
she couldn't accept that. . . .
We've been separated for over a year now. We see each other
from time to time, and Meg has hopes that eventually we'll be
together again. I don't share that hope.
I should never have married. I can see that now. . . .

Another source of conflict, one frequently reported by gay
women, is dissatisfaction with the restrictive roles of married
life. As **Harriet**, thirty-two, explains:

Being a housekeeper, wife, nursemaid, and cook didn't suit
me. I tried, but I never felt I succeeded. I felt trapped, a
prisoner of chintz and nappies, with a lifetime of dusting,
cooking, cleaning, and washing ahead of me. . . .
When Jerry was born, my feelings became incredibly mixed. I
was happy and miserable all at once. And after a year I was
largely miserable again, because there seemed no escape. I
felt I couldn't cope. I didn't *wish* to cope. I wanted 'out'.
Yet for three years I carried on as before. I tried to be a good
mother, a good housekeeper, a good wife. It seems I had no
time to be myself. All my energies were exhausted in helping
others, and keeping things tidy for them.
Finally, when Jerry was about three years old, I met Isobel.
This was at the same time that I started evening classes. I
wanted to get away from the house, really.
Andy wasn't too happy about my classes because it meant his
having to stay at home with Jerry. He felt rather put out, and
told me I was shirking my responsibilities.
Isobel and I hit it off straight away. She was in much the same
situation as I. So we had something in common to begin with
. . . there's no 'happy ending', though. Isobel and I are still
friends, not lovers. There's not much likelihood of the
relationship developing on another level.
Andy was always resentful of Isobel, though. That *did* upset
me, and one evening I just lashed out at him with all my pent-
up feelings and frustrations. I told him what I owed to Isobel,
that she had brought me out and helped me to see myself as I
am. . . .
Andy nearly hit the roof. He threatened to take Jerry away,
saying I wasn't any good for him. Which wasn't true. I love

Jerry. It's just that everything was getting on top of me. . . .
Andy soon moved out of the bedroom and slept on the couch.
After a few weeks he calmed down. And then, quite suddenly,
he moved out. Without a word. There was a note on the
kitchen table one morning. It said: 'Dad (Andy's father) will
have collected us by the time you read this. Will be in touch.'
And now, of course, it's in the courts.

Gay Mothers: A Court Case

It was Andy, rather than Harriet, who was given the custody of
Jerry. This is not at all unusual. In the majority of cases where
the mother is known to be lesbian, the father is given custody of
the child. This fact is borne out in a recent court case[3] in which a
mother's application for custody of her seven-year-old
daughter was denied after the father, who had since remarried,
protested that his former wife was living with another woman 'in
a lesbian relationship'. Although the judge agreed that the child
had been well looked after, and a psychiatrist, called in as a
character witness, recommended that the mother be given the
custody of the child (which was also the child's wish), the view
from the Bench was that the mother was lacking in 'femininity',
i.e. that she possessed a strong personality and refused to
'sacrifice her lesbian proclivities' for the sake of the child.

The judge concluded that homosexuality was unnatural. The
child, he felt, would be the recipient of 'unhealthy attitudes' if
left with the mother, and would also be left vulnerable to the
taunts of friends. Although the father was said to be 'less
intelligent' than his former wife, the judge was satisfied that he
possessed 'hard-working habits'. His new wife, who had made a
favourable impression on the judge, had helped the court to
conclude that the child would have a happier and healthier life if
the father was given custody, care, and control.

This particular case was never taken to the Court of Appeal
because the mother's barrister persuaded her that such a course
of action was hopeless. It would not be possible to persuade the
Appeal Court that the judge's decision ought to be reversed, the
barrister informed her. In view of current custody laws, one
might regard this as realistic advice. Courts decide what is in the
child's best interests, and the child's 'best interests' are reckoned
on the basis of conventional middle-class standards. Hence,

though the courts 'would probably not feel', as Anna Coote has
pointed out, 'that a child should be protected from the corrupt
atmosphere of a stately home with a full contingent of servants
or freed from the repressive influence of a strict religious
upbringing',[4] it would (as we have seen) protect a child from a
mother who was thought to be lacking in 'femininity'.

A Gay Father

Gay fathers also suffer from conventional ideas about what
constitutes a 'good parent'. **Lawrence** is the twenty-nine-year-
old father of an eight-year-old daughter by a marriage which
recently ended in divorce. He speaks here of some of the answers
he gave to his daughter's questions concerning his relationship
with a male lover:

> You don't hear many gay fathers tell their stories, do you?
> Until I joined a group of gay fathers, about a year ago, I had
> no contact with others in my situation. I had no idea about
> how they managed to deal with the questions of their
> children. . . .
> The questions can be tricky. But, really, if you're honest with
> your kid, they're not difficult to answer. Let me give just one
> example. A few weeks ago Kit, my daughter, was dropped off
> at the flat by her mother. Jon, my lover, was in the kitchen, in
> his pyjamas, putting together a late breakfast.
> We had been expecting Kit, but Jon was a bit anxious. He had
> never met Kit before, though he had heard me talk about her
> a great deal. . . .
> After Kit had tucked away an egg, an orange drink, and three
> slices of toast, she looked over at Jon for a long, long minute.
> Then, turning towards me, she asked: 'Who do you love the
> most in the world, Mum or Jon?'
> I said that I loved them both in different ways. I loved her
> mother with one kind of love which I wasn't able to give to
> Jon or to anybody else; and that I loved Jon with another kind
> of love which belonged to him and him alone.
> 'And other men? Do you love other men besides Jon?' she
> asked.
> I thought about that for a moment, and then said, yes, I did.
> 'Why?' she asked. 'Because', I said, 'loving people is

something I've learned to do very well, something I hope I'm very good at.'

Kit thought about that for a few seconds, and then said, 'All right; so long as there's enough left over for me.'

A lot of people think that the child suffers from the knowledge of a parent's homosexuality. These people don't give children much credit . . . I didn't have to go into any lengthy expositions about gays, or homosexuality, or any of the rest of it.

I'm certain, however, that Kit *understands* at a feeling level, and that's good enough, for the present. I was honest with her. She knows who I am, and she loves me. That means more than the silly things some people might say about gays.

Resolving Marital Conflicts

Although many homosexuals choose to separate from their heterosexual partners as a way of resolving the conflicts and strains of marriage, there are several other modes of adjustment with which the counsellor should be familiar. The first of these is a platonic atangement, as described by **Sam**:

We stress the non-sexual side of our relationship. Don't laugh when I say it, but we're 'good friends'. You might say Plato's been our guide.

Look at it this way: we've been married eighteen years. Joy was nineteen and I was twenty when we married. So we've spent nearly half our lives together. You don't separate easily after so long together. I doubt if I could be as happy with anyone else.

Joy and I have careers. We enjoy our work, *love it!* That means a great deal to us. We're people who love to work. We also have many outside interests . . . hobbies, and so on. . . .

I've had many affairs with men, almost all of them short-lived. That's the sort of person I am. The last affair I had was almost a year ago. Joy? I don't know. We never talk about our affairs, our sexual affairs. . . . Why should we? As long as they don't cause problems. . . .

Another form of adjustment is the 'open marriage'—one in which both partners tolerate the existence of extra-marital sexual relationships. As **Lydia**, a writer, aged fifty, explains:

The most successful marriages are those in which each of the partners respects the other's needs and wishes. . . .

Angus and I have what they call, nowadays, an 'open marriage'. Neither of us prevents the other from growing in our own special way. . . .

We have three children, all grown up, living away from home; two are married. They know I'm bisexual. They accept it. That's the way we brought them up: to be tolerant, accepting kids. . . .

It's odd. I have the deep love of my children, and yet my children, in the past, have often been obstacles to the love of other women. Lesbians will stereotype me as 'heterosexual mother/wife'. If you are a bisexual, or a married gay, you're something of a sexual pariah. Perhaps it's changing now. But I remember when it was very difficult for the bisexual to relate to the gay scene. It was the biggest 'problem' of all. . . .

Why did I get married? I loved Angus. I never had a woman lover before marrying. I don't know if being more experienced, sexually, would have made a difference. Angus and I were in love, and we wanted to affirm our relationship in some way. Angus saw marriage as a mature statement of our commitment to each other, the supporting bond of our relationship. I went along with that. I still do.

Some of my friends say it's 'politically incorrect', marriage, that you shouldn't seek validation from society for your relationship. I can't agree, though. I don't see anything wrong in using social institutions to shore you up, if that's what you need. If institutions can be of help in making you happier and stronger, then use them.

Of course, marriage *has* been corrupted, but I don't know that *in itself* it is corrupt. There's a potential there for supporting, as well as controlling. It's not the *only* arrangement for people in love. It's only one of many.

You can, of course, make yourself a victim of marriage if you choose to. I think, though, that I'm one of its beneficiaries. Then again, Angus and I are perhaps a bit special. We have an open marriage: marriage is what *we* want it to be.

Of all the means of resolving a marital conflict so far considered, the 'open marriage' would appear to be the most 'successful'. It is also the most rare, depending as it does on the sexual versatility of the one partner and the broadmindedness of the other. Less happy variations of this and the platonic arrangement are more usual, and it is these that the counsellor will most frequently encounter. The anti-gay bias of our culture induces gays to marry, but then prevents their mutual acceptance of each other in marriage. This is a situation that must be viewed in the light of our religious views of homosexual behaviour, which is one of the concerns of my next chapter.

Summary

In this chapter I have considered the situation of married gays. There are four basic reasons for gays choosing to enter into such a seemingly conflicting situation as heterosexual marriage: first, insufficient awareness of one's gayness at the time of marriage (**Judith**); second, a conscious desire to escape from the knowledge of one's gayness (**Toby**); third, rational choice (**Arthur**); fourth, social and familial pressures (**Edward**; **Cheryl**).

In most cases, the heterosexual spouse is not aware of his or her partner's homosexuality (**Flo**), either because the gay person is not fully conscious of being homosexual at the time of marriage, or because the gay person chooses to keep his or her homosexuality a secret. There are also cases, however, in which the heterosexual spouse takes the decision to marry in the full knowledge that the partner is homosexual. The motives here are (1) love; (2) the hope of a change taking place in the sexual orientation of the gay partner; and (3) the belief that the factor of homosexuality is insignificant to the success of the marriage.

Conflicts often develop in such marriages due to waning sexual attraction; the development of outside relationships (**Vincent**); and dissatisfaction with the restrictive roles of married life (**Harriet**). When couples with children decide to split up, the gay parent is, in law, at a distinct disadvantage, since the custody laws operate according to conventional middle-class standards (**A Court Case** and **Lawrence**).

Not all homosexuals choose separation or divorce as their means of resolving marital conflicts, however. At least two other forms of adjustment are fairly commonplace: a platonic arrangement in which the non-sexual side of the relationship is developed (**Sam**), and an open marriage in which both partners tolerate the existence of extra-marital sexual relationships (**Lydia**). In general, though, less happy variations of these two adjustments are pursued.

5
Gay Sex, Straight Religion

JESUS CHRIST

WANTED: For Sedition, Criminal Anarchy, Crimes against Nature, Vagrancy and Conspiracy to Overthrow all Established Governments by Revolutionary Love.

Dresses poorly. Said to be a Carpenter by trade. Ill-nourished. Has visionary ideas of establishing a free and loving society. Associates with common working people, national and racial minorities, the unemployed, and prostitutes. Is often to be found in the company of twelve other highly suspicious men, one of whom, John by name, he calls his Beloved. Alias: 'Prince of Peace', 'Son of Humanity'. 'Servant of the People'. Bearded. Dark-skinned. Marks on hands and feet as the result of injuries inflicted by an angry mob led by bankers, generals, church officials, educators and other respectable citizens and legal authorities.

—from the Summer 1975 *Calendar* of The People's Church: Community of the Love of Christ (New York City)

Sex versus Faith: Five Cases

Opposition to homosexuality is closely bound up with the nature of our Judaeo-Christian heritage. Counsellors will therefore need to know what advice is appropriate for gays whose religious beliefs appear to be in conflict with their sexual orientation. Such advice depends, in part, upon counsellors' familiarity with those passages of Scripture and their inter-pretation which have traditionally been used to legitimize the oppression of gays. These passages, along with present church attitudes on homosexuality, will be considered below. To begin with, let us listen to five voices, each of which illustrates one or more aspects of possible conflict between homosexuality and faith. The first belongs to **Deidre**, sixteen, who writes:

I am only sixteen years of age, but I am as certain as I can be that I am a lesbian. I am not happy about this because I know that in the eyes of God I am a sinner. It says so in the Bible. I have read the Bible through and through and everywhere (homosexuality) is condemned. You can check this if you like, as I know exactly where it is, it is 1 Corinthians 6.9. There are other places in the Bible, not only Corinthians, and if you would like to know where then I will tell you in my next letter. The list is long. . . .

What I want to know from you is, does this mean that I will go to hell, or will it make a difference if I marry, like other girls? Please give me the answers to these questions, because there is no one else to whom I dare to turn for help. I am asking you even though I think I know the answer. . . .

I am so worried, I cannot tell you. Inside I feel a nothing. Sometimes I want to hide myself when I have bad thoughts but I know how silly that is, to think that you can run away; you can't.

Please, write. You are the first person I have ever told anything, and though you are someone I have never met, already I feel I know you.

Love,

Deidre

If Deidre had been troubled by any other moral issue, she might well have taken it to some responsible member of her church. But because of the expected traditional attitudes of the church towards homosexuality, she felt unable to share her anxieties and doubts with a fellow Christian. Why is this the usual course of action when the issue involved is homosexuality? After all, it stands to reason that if those to whom one generally turns in time of distress are thought likely to be sympathetic, gays like Deidre would not hesitate to share with them their doubts and worries. If, on the other hand, there exists only a condemnatory attitude, then gays may well isolate themselves, perhaps for ever, from those whose very ministry it is to be of help.

The fear of having one's confidence greeted by icy disapproval has forced many gays to question the very foundations of their faith. A counselling group which I once facilitated consisted of twelve gays, including myself. Of this number, ten had been raised in the Christian faith, and two in the Jewish. Yet not one person in twelve could honestly say that his or her religion had offered any significant support during those periods when faith and sexual orientation seemed most in conflict. Some of us had sought help and been rebuffed. Others were fearful of seeking help owing to the 'bad experience' of friends, or because the church's attitude on homosexuality was already all too clear to us.

Lorraine, one of the twelve members of this counselling group, spoke for several others when she said:

I left the church because I wasn't accepted as a lesbian. It took me a long time to understand this, but, once I did, there was no alternative except to leave. It was that simple. . . .

I would say that the real crisis came when I met Margo. We attended the same church. Our religious convictions were very much the same. We love each other very much, and when we first discovered these feelings, we wanted to share them with others in the church.

Any hopes we may have had that friends in the church would accept us were soon dashed. We're both very sociable people. We like to entertain. Before we moved in together, we were invited into people's homes fairly frequently, for dinner, drinks, parties. . . .

Once we set up house together, everything changed. Not dramatically, but in subtle ways. We weren't invited out so often, and only rarely would we *both* receive an invitation to someone's home. . . .

I spoke to the vicar about this. He listened, and when I was finished he thanked me for sharing with him my 'problem' (as he chose to call it) and then, very firmly, and at considerable length, informed me that, given the generally unsophisticated views which *other* people held on this 'sensitive subject', it wasn't altogether surprising that people should behave as I described.

This was followed by a brief sermon, during the course of which I was informed that being a lesbian wasn't exactly a sin, but that homosexual acts were wrong in the sense that they made 'unnatural' use of sexual organs—sexual organs whose proper use was restricted to heterosexual marriage.

Well, I'm sorry to say that this exchange marked a turning-point in my relationship with the church. For years I had worn blinkers. I wouldn't allow myself to see the hypocrisy of some of my fellow Christians. I was afraid to face up to facts. I knew what might happen if I *did* face up to facts. . . .

The church seems split on this issue of homosexuality. . . . It refuses to take a stand. It does nothing substantial for fear of alienating its members. . . .

In refusing to lead the way, it's lost my respect. . . .

Not everyone who joins a counselling group or who contacts a gay organization seeks help with an immediate problem. There are many gays like **Lorraine** who, as she says,

. . . would simply like to meet other gays as a way of renewing that sense of *belonging* to others, or to a community. This is something I feel I've lost since leaving the church. In coming together with other gays who are also trying to raise their level of consciousness, I'm hoping to recover that sense of sharing goals and commitments. . . . By exchanging feelings and experiences, I feel that I've come much, much closer to understanding myself and others. It's been very stimulating. I've been made aware of possibilities in my life that I never knew existed.

Lorraine's disillusionment with the church springs from a sense of being rejected by her fellow Christians. This feeling was once shared by **Paul**, thirty-two. Although in recent years he has managed to reconcile his homosexuality with the teachings of his church, he was once deeply troubled by feelings of guilt. As he explains:

At first I found it impossible to be both a 'practising' homosexual and a 'practising' Christian. At age twenty I was confirmed as a member of my church. At that time I promised I would not again receive communion if I had sexual relations with another man. I kept that promise for over three years. For the next two years I had occasional sexual experiences and always felt guilty about it. Then I met Malcolm, and for the next six years I had sex exclusively with him. I lost all feelings of guilt and at the same time became more open to others and more involved in the church. Slowly I forgot that there was ever a contradiction between my sexual preferences and the teachings of the church. Of course my church is not as rigid on this matter as some other branches of the church are. There is, for example, an organization of gays who are working for a better understanding with the churches, and they seem, slowly, to be working out a reconciliation of sorts. I do believe that it is possible for a homosexual to be a sincere and faithful Christian. Just as fathers or mothers care for each of their children, so I believe that God cares for each person. This holds even if a person is not exactly like the majority (like a member of the family that is not exactly like all the other children).

Moreover, God calls all his children to reconciliation, and he exhorts each of us to use what abilities we have both for our own good and the good of others. Regardless of what we are, I believe that God will use us to the extent that we will allow him to do so. . . .

The churches are slowly coming to this point of view, and there will probably be more drastic changes in my lifetime. This is what I pray for. . . .

The sense of guilt which Paul experienced is one which most gays will readily understand. In some cases, such as that of **Olga**, twenty-six, feelings of guilt are exacerbated by a morally scrupulous nature weaned on the sexually oppressive attitudes of people around her:

I was born in Sheffield, but my memories of the place are bleak. Until recently these were my only memories: Sheffield, the home I was born in, the church and schools I attended for more than ten years. . . .

My home was like a church. Evenings, Dad read chapters from the Bible. I remember having nightmares. Dad read half a book each night, and then expounded on several passages. He had a great reverence for family life, my father, and he dwelt a great deal on 'crimes' that marred the sanctity of the family unit. I particularly remember the passages dealing with sexual impurity. Several times I became ill after readings from Leviticus or Deuteronomy. . . .

All this must have greatly inhibited me in ways that, even now, I don't fully understand. . . .

After school I went to secretarial college, and then to university. My father thought university a bad idea for a woman. His grumblings became so insistent that, after a year, I decided to leave. I took a job as an editorial assistant in a publishing house. I quite enjoyed that. . . .

When I was twenty-four, my father died. He had been ill for two years, and his dying was long and painful. Within eight months of my father's death, my mother died. Her heart stopped beating one night. . . . I remember how lonely I felt, how lost and stranded.

There was this boy, Geoff, whom I had known since we were children. He was a great favourite with my parents. He was studying for the ministry. My parents always hoped I'd marry him. He was always asking me to marry him. When my parents died, I said yes.

It was crazy. You see, I hadn't yet convinced myself that I am lesbian. No, that's not right. It would be more true to say that I was too terrified to even think of such a thing. And that meant not thinking about my sexual identity at all. . . .

Two weeks before the wedding was to take place, I called it off. Something happened which I'm ashamed even now to talk about. . . . I knew this girl, a friend, and she seemed to know me better than I did. She told me that I was marrying Geoff to fill a gap left by my parent's death. And then she said: 'I expect you're a latent homosexual.'

It was awful! She told me straight out, in the most unfeeling way imaginable. . . .

I put the house on the market, sold everything, quit my job. I said goodbye to Geoff, then packed my bags and left for London. Just like that! Everyone thought I had gone mad. Perhaps I had. Perhaps, too, I had finally come to my senses. My original motive was to put as much distance as possible between myself and my friend. Or, if you like, between myself and the truth. Yet one of the first things I did on arriving in London was to confide in the vicar of the church near the flat I had rented. He wanted to be helpful, I could tell. He said he had little experience in this area but recommended a gay women's organization. He thought they could probably help me. I followed it up. I went there and attended these weekly discussion groups. At first I was too nervous and shy to speak.

The other women were so open in discussing the most intimate matters. But I was far too inhibited, so I stopped attending after two meetings.

Two months went by and I decided to go back again—more out of loneliness than anything else. Whatever motive, I'm pleased now that I did return.

I managed to talk about myself in a way I had never done before, particularly about my fears, and sex. It was good for me to talk about these feelings, to share them . . . and very exciting, very creative. . . .

No one laughed when I told them how my mother had long ago said that sex between a man and a woman was sinful if the motive was pleasure. . . . I never saw my parents show any physical affection for one another, *never*. . . .

I told them about a teacher at school who warned us against masturbation. I'm certain the teacher saw me blush. She said that masturbation 'saddened God' because the body was a 'sacred vessel' that should never be polluted by 'self-lust'.

She was also the first person to mention love between women. 'Such women are lesbians', I can remember her saying—it was said with a sort of hissing sound attached to the word 'lesbians'. These women, she said, were an 'abomination', and were condemned in the Scriptures. . . .

All the girls seemed horrified that lesbians might be walking the streets of Sheffield. Afterwards, oh, for *months* and *months* afterwards, if girls happened to be standing close to one another, or if any two girls were special friends—you know, seen together a great deal—there would always be someone close to hand who would shout 'lesbian'.

During those last two years at school, I remember that 'lesbian' was the most rude and hurtful word you could possibly use against another girl.

It's funny, though. When this teacher used the word 'lesbian'—the way she said it—I seemed at once, at that very moment, to understand *everything*. And, just as quickly, something deep inside—something unconscious, I guess —seemed determined that I should *forget* everything.

Growing up lesbian in a heterosexual environment can be very alienating. Only in exceptional cases do parents or teachers pause to consider the possibility that a child or student might be homosexual. Thus, some gays, like Olga, will listen in silence as others speak belittlingly of an aspect of their personality which is absolutely crucial to their sense of self.

Stan, a twenty-six-year-old post-graduate student, is Jewish. His memories of being excluded are no less intense than those of Olga.

The problems faced by Jewish gays are different only in emphasis from those of Christians. . . .

One thing a Jew is always conscious of is his Jewishness. It's the product of 2000 years of persecution. Oppressed peoples have long memories. Jewish institutions help to preserve and perpetuate those memories. The best example of this is the family. Jews are fiercely proud and protective of the family unit.

You can trace this Jewish pride in the family way back to ancient times. In the Jewish struggle for survival, barrenness was a curse. It was vital to the survival of the small Jewish tribes that they increase and multiply. Homosexuality was therefore shunned as subversive to the procreative function of sex and a threat to family life. . . . These attitudes continue, though twentieth-century society is very different. . . .

Religion was an integral part of family life in our home. I never realized until I was an adult that you could actually separate the two. From the moment I was born, I found myself being initiated into a ghetto mentality: circumcision, religious training, Bar Mitzvah and manhood!

And then, of course, dating 'nice Jewish girls' and preparing for marriage and a family of my own. . . .

My mother was as much the matriarch as any of those caricatures we're all so familiar with. In the novels of Philip Roth, for example, or in the jokes of Jewish comedians. Mother ruled the roost. She made absolutely certain that family ties were maintained, religion reverenced, etc., etc., etc.

Mother also acted as a sort of non-unionized marriage broker. 'Shirley, she's a nice girl', she'd say to me. 'What's the matter, you don't like nice girls?' And if it wasn't Shirley, it was Sara, or Naomi, or Miriam. . . .

It's still difficult for young Jews to break out of this mould.
The problems are enormous. Like other guys, I grew up
believing my gay difference was unique. Everything
reinforced this conviction, particularly the stress on marriage,
and the religious beliefs deeply embedded in my Jewish
heritage that I was conditioned into since I was a small
boy. . . .

Despite the story of David and Jonathan, I come from a
religious background which suggests I don't really exist. If
you don't believe this, you have only to look in the 1971
edition of *The Encyclopedia Judaica*. What you find there is truly
astonishing; for example, the author of the entry on
'homosexuality' speaks of a 'virtual absence' of gays or of the
'rare incidence' of gays among Jews! Now this just isn't true!
Yet even Maimonides followed the Talmud in holding that
Jews are 'not suspect to practise homosexuality'.

So you can see how far back this myth goes. Talmudic law
makes homosexual relations a capital offence (just as in
Leviticus) and is based on the general warning not to indulge
in the 'abhorrent practices' of the Egyptians and the
Canaanites. . . . Believe me, the situation is scarcely better
today. The Progressives are only *slightly* more sympathetic
than the Orthodox wing. . . .

It wasn't until I prised myself loose from the heterosexual
embrace of my family and synagogue that I was able to *even
begin* to come to terms with the reality of being gay. It was then
that I realized, as never before, how very much of a
disappointment I was going to be both to my parents and to
my religion.

Our culture is one in which most individuals derive some clues
as to who they are from the faith into which they were born. This
being the case, any religion which is intolerant of homosexuality
may therefore be encouraging gays like Deidre, Lorraine, Olga,
Paul, and Stan to develop a self-image characterized by terms
such as 'sinner', 'a source of scandal', 'dishonourable',
'unnatural', 'abomination', 'abhorrent'.

Homosexuality and Scripture

Such terms as these reflect an opposition to homosexuality that is closely bound up with the nature of our Judaeo-Christian heritage. Hence, many of today's Christians (and Jews) are victims of a condemnatory view of homosexuality that is deeply rooted in the Old Testament and perpetuated by the New.[1] Unfortunately, the use of Scriptures to condemn homosexuality—a tendency which exhibits many of the worst possible features of uncritical biblical exegesis—is still practised as a means of oppressing gay people.[2] This being the case, the counsellor will need to be familiar with the principal biblical texts employed to censure gays. There are six: three from Pentateuch and three from the Pauline epistles.

The Sodom and Gomorrah story (Gen. 19.1–28) is often viewed as the *locus classicus* of divine wrath against homosexual behaviour. It was the Code of Justinian which first alluded to 'the most reprehensible vices and . . . *crimes contrary to nature* . . . [which] incur the just anger of God, and bring about *the destruction of cities* along with their inhabitants' [emphasis added].[3] This reference to Sodom and Gomorrah is of crucial significance for Western law codes dealing with homosexuality. The Justinian Code was the model used by legal students at Bologna when Roman law was revived in Europe in the eleventh century and is, therefore, the progenitor of a legal tradition dating back some 900 years.

Notwithstanding this fact, the story of Sodom and Gomorrah remains much less a product of history than of folklore and legend. This is the same story, let us not forget, wherein women are transferred into salt; men are struck blind by angels; and two cities of Palestine are destroyed by apparent volcanic eruptions in an area of the world where volcanoes have never been recorded.

It is also true that when Old Testament writers such as Isaiah, Jeremiah, Ezekiel, Amos, and Zephaniah speak of Sodom, as they frequently do, they make no reference whatsoever to homosexuality. Thus, the prophet Ezekiel, speaking more as a socialist than as a fundamentalist, interprets the sin of Sodom and Gomorrah not as homosexuality but, rather, as luxury, idleness, and lack of concern for the poor. Indeed, it was only at the beginning of the Christian era, about 2000 years after the events were supposed to have taken place, that the Sodom story became, as Lewis Williams points out, 'the vehicle for anti-homosexual propaganda in the hands of Jewish philosophers and historians who were in revolt against Hellenic manners'.[4]

If the Sodom and Gomorrah story is a fanciful medley of fact and fiction, the Levitican code is depressingly clear. It is here that we read: 'Thou shalt not lie with mankind as with womankind; it is an abomination' (Lev. 18.22); 'If a man also lie with mankind as he lieth with woman, both of them have committed an abomination; they shall surely be put to death, their blood shall be upon them' (Lev. 20.13).

Such prohibitions as these will doubtless prove disturbing to many gays. It might be helpful to remember, then, that these are but two injunctions falling within a very complex series of prohibitions which, were one to use the same process of random selection as in the case of homosexuality, could lead to theologies of food (Lev. 11.10–12; 17.10; 19.26), clothing (19.19), and hairdressing (19.27) that would cause havoc with many of our present cultural patterns.

Yet some will still insist that the injunctions cited against homosexuality are clear and incontestable. Let us assume, for the sake of argument, that this is true. In that case, other prohibitions found in Leviticus are no less clear and incontestable, e.g., that which requires adulterers to be put to death (20.10). Of course, we reject the latter injunction, which refers to *heterosexual* relationships, but accept the former, which refers to *homosexual* relationships. What is it that enables some to say that certain laws of God are obsolete while others should remain operative? The answer, it seems to me, is that each religious group claims its own version of the truth, and that each of us, in turn, decides between contending viewpoints by a process of personal judgement. When it suits our purposes we change, modify, and reinterpret the law. Thus, we may decide that adultery is not to be punished by death, but that homosexuality should still be regarded as an abomination.

Still others will argue that the advent of Christianity has imperceptibly brought about a rejection of many Old Testament commandments. Let us turn to the New Testament, then, and consider briefly the Pauline epistles. There are two passages of special relevance:

> For this cause God gave them up unto vile affections: for even their women did change the natural use into that which is against nature: and likewise also the men, leaving the natural use of the women, burned in their lust one towards another; men with them working that which is unseemly, and receiving in themselves that recompense of their error which was meet (Rom. 1.26–7).

> Know ye not that the unrighteous shall not inherit the kingdom of God? Be not deceived: neither fornicators, nor idolaters, nor adulterers, nor effeminate, nor abusers of themselves with mankind . . . shall inherit the kingdom of God (1 Cor. 6.9–10).

Perhaps the most important point to be made about Paul's two statements on homosexuality[5] and his comments on other sexual ethics is that they constitute a direct reflection of his Jewish background and must be seen in that context. Being a product of his time, Paul associated homosexuality with the tendency to idolatry and heresy. In neither of the above passages does he attempt to deal with the morality of homosexuality as a human condition but, rather, as a deviation from the religious practice which made of Judaism the monolith that had withstood the infiltration of Canaanite, Babylonian, Greek, and Roman influences. Thus, in *Homosexuality and the Western Christian Tradition*, Derrick Sherwin Bailey has argued that Romans 1.26–7 and 1 Corinthians 6.9–10 must be interpreted as 'the Christian reaction to the dissolute sexual behaviour of the Hellenistic world, which was regarded as the inevitable concomitant of idolatry'.[6]

For Paul, then, *all* sexuality was suspect.[7] His condemnation of homosexuality, as Rattray Taylor has pointed out,[8] was simply one aspect of the general condemnation of all sexual activity which was not directly necessary to the races. Hence, in Romans 1.18 we read that 'the wrath of God is revealed from heaven against *all* ungodliness and unrighteousness of men' [emphasis added]. Indeed, it sometimes appears that for Paul the most Christian society imaginable was one in which all men remained bachelors, just as he did, and completely abstained from sexual relations. 'It is good for a man', Paul remarks in 1 Corinthians 7.1, 'not to touch a woman.' But if the 'unmarried . . . cannot contain themselves', then, says the apostle, 'let them marry; for it is better to marry than to burn' (1 Cor. 7.8–9). Though even here, within marriage, one must add, severe restrictions were imposed on sexual relations, the husband and wife being admonished to give themselves over to 'fasting and prayer' (1 Cor. 7.5).

These teachings of the Bible, when combined with the moral theology of St Augustine, constitute the main weights of Christian doctrinal tradition against homosexuality. This tradition, in its interpretation of the fundamental purpose of the sexual drive as procreation, and in its classification of sexual acts as 'natural' and 'unnatural', has militated against the full acceptance of the homosexual. Gays are still regarded by many in the churches as a threat to family life—a belief which has often led to outright condemnation of homosexual acts and relationships. Still others within the churches, while more amenable to a greater toleration of homosexuality, are anxious lest any re-examination of the issue should lead to questions concerning all other canons of sexual morals. It is this worrying possibility of an extension of the subject into a much broader area of Christian sexual ethics which may well pose the principal obstacle to full acceptance by the churches of several million homosexuals.

The Gospel of Love

While recognizing that counsellors must abide by their own religious convictions, it is possible to offer helpful advice to gays who are troubled by scriptural prohibitions without compromising one's own moral principles or imposing exclusively Judaeo-Christian ethics on others. For example, counsellors might stress the fact that the authors of the Scriptures interpreted their faith in terms of the world in which they lived. Many modern churchmen, on the other hand, are convinced that contemporary morality should not be based on ancient rules as interpreted by medieval scholars but, rather, on the basis of all the insights and discoveries made available to us over the past 2000 years. It might also be helpful to remind gays that the overwhelming majority of religions outside the Judaeo-Christian tradition are largely unconcerned with matters of sexual morality; hence, such proscriptions against homosexuality as do exist reflect philosophical convictions that are entirely subjective.[9]

But most important of all, the counsellor might remind gays of the gospel of love in action. Christians could look to the ministry of Christ, where one finds no direct references to the subject of homosexuality, Jesus preferring to restrict his very occasional pronouncements on sexual matters to guidelines and standards for use in human relationships. Indeed, the moral teachings of Christ regarding sexual expression are just as adaptable to homosexuals as they are to heterosexuals. After all, it was Jesus who reminded us that 'God so loved the world, that He gave His only begotten Son, that whosoever believeth in Him should not perish, but have everlasting life.' He did not qualify this by adding 'but with the exception of homosexuals'.

When we stop to consider the ways in which this gospel of love is communicated in our contemporary world, we find that the churches reflect a very broad spectrum of theological views on homosexuality. To begin with, the Jewish faith holds that homosexuality frustrates the procreative purpose of sex; it does 'damage to family life'; and it constitutes 'an unnatural perversion, debasing the dignity of man'. Jewish teaching firmly rejects notions of homosexuality as an illness or as something which is morally neutral, although this latter view has gained some support among contemporary moralists. Generally speaking, Jews appear to regard the more liberal attitudes found in certain modern Christian circles as possibly due to the exaggerated importance Christians have traditionally accorded the term 'love'. But Jewish law, according to one influential writer on the subject, holds that 'no hedonistic ethic, even if called "love", can justify the morality of homosexuality any more than it can legitimize adultery, incest, or polygamy, however genuinely such acts may be performed out of love and by mutual consent.'[10]

The most monolithic position on homosexuality is taken by the Roman Catholic Church. In considering the morality of this sexual orientation, the Catholic Church makes a distinction between responsibility for the homosexual 'condition'; the objective morality of the homosexual act; and the subjective responsibility of individual gays for particular acts.[11] According to Father John Kane, author of *What is Homosexuality?*, there is no doubt that homosexual acts are 'objectively sinful' in all cases. However, the 'subjective guilt' of the individual is less easily determined since this depends on each gay person's 'total personality structure'.[12]

Father John F. Harvey, whose writings on homosexuality have received wide circulation within the Catholic Church, has advised counsellors to direct homosexuals to undertake a course of psychotherapy which would 'change the direction of their instincts'. Those individuals who feel they are too old for such therapy, or those who are otherwise unable to pursue such a course of treatment, should be advised to follow 'an ascetical plan of life if they desire to be fully human and Christian'. An element of proven worth within such a programme, says Harvey, is 'the actual performance of apostolic and charitable work . . . [rather] than the achievement of satisfactory sexual relationships'.[13]

Finally, a recent document entitled *Declaration on Certain Questions Concerning Sexual Ethics* issued by the Sacred Congregation for the Doctrine of the Faith (the former Holy Office) firmly opposes any relaxation of the Roman Catholic Church's traditional rejection of homosexuality. Drafted by an international group of moral theologians with the approval and confirmation of Pope Paul VI, who ordered its publication, this document advises the faithful that 'homosexual acts are intrinsically disordered and can in no case be approved of'. It further adds that 'in sacred Scripture [such acts] are condemned as a serious depravity and even presented as the sad consequence of rejecting God.'[14]

The Protestant Churches offer a much broader range of opinion. As far as the Anglican Church is concerned, Kenneth Leech claims that it has 'come a long way since the late Archbishop Fisher could say that "homosexuality is a shameful vice and a grievous sin from which deliverance is to be sought by every means".'[15] Issues once swept under the rug or pushed out of sight are slowly being brought into the open. Thus, in 1973, the Archbishop of Canterbury, Dr Coggan, who was then Archbishop of York, urged that the Anglican Church should accept rather than ostracize homosexuals.[16] And, indeed, within certain sections of the Church of England there even appears to be an acceptance of the validity of gay love.

Hope for the Future

Although religious groups are far from anxious to reconsider the subject of homosexuality, many individuals within the churches are now urging a reassessment of traditional attitudes. Some of these critics are themselves gay, and they argue that condemnation of homosexuality inhibits personal and religious development. Others tend to see the issue in the light of sexual ethics, while still others regard it as, quite simply, a question of justice.

Such critics as these are determined that the subject of homosexuality should find a permanent place on the Christian agenda. They have already met with some success. Both the Unitarians and the Social Responsibility Council of the Society of Friends have now published studies on homosexuality. The former group has posed the question of whether society or the churches are justified in expecting gays to abstain permanently from any physical expression of love and affection for their own sex. The Quaker study raises the same question, and offers an 'inside' account of homosexuality as a basis for future discussion.

Periodicals have also contributed to the emerging debate by occasionally devoting space in their columns to those wishing an exchange of views on the possible sources of conflict between gays and their faith. In the last few years *Christian Renewal*, an ecumenical journal, has printed articles and letters by laity and clergy seeking a re-examination of the churches' traditional stance on homosexuality in the light of our new understanding of sexuality.

An Anglican commission on homosexuality was recently set up to review the Church's position on homosexuality, and REACH, an interdenominational organization, has been formed to assist the Church in its understanding and support of gays. In addition, various ecumenical communities such as the Universal Fellowship and the Metropolitan Community Church have been established. These groups are open to all, but with a special interest in, and concern for, Christian gays. A group of

Catholic homosexuals called QUEST has also been formed, and this aims to reconcile the Church's moral theology with an acceptance of homosexuality. In line with this objective, Father Fabian Cowper, OSB, in a recent issue of *Christian Renewal*, has given his support to a claim made by a number of distinguished Continental theologians that 'natural law' has been based on outdated conceptions of nature and that moral theology should concern itself not simply with acts, but also with the spirit and values which motivate gays in their lifestyles and relationships.[17]

According to Lewis Williams, a contributor to a recent collection of essays on ethics, theology, and homosexuality, one of the churches' top priorities must be the development of 'a theology of engagement aimed at undoing the effects of two thousand years of religious anti-homosexualism'.[18] The Revd Thomas Maurer, writing in the same volume, agrees with this, and argues for a theology that will spring from 'one's experience, and out of one's own visceral being'.[19]

But if the churches are to evolve such a theology they must begin with the premise that no sexual orientation is superior to any other. Such an assumption of equality should extend to the realm of moral responsibility, too—an acknowledgement of the fact that homosexuals are no less responsible for their sexual lives than are heterosexuals. After all, true religion recognizes that sexual maturity and self-realization are essential parts of the gospel of wholeness preached by Judaism and Christianity alike. Such tensions as arise derive from the historical attitudes towards homosexuality and the modern interpretation of sexual fulfilment as a Christian way of life. Those churches which contribute to the oppression of gays by regarding homosexuality as a sin need to be persuaded that such an attitude produces many of the very evils which they so vociferously condemn. This is a point which is forcefully made in a pamphlet entitled *Towards a Quaker View of Sex*:[20]

> Sexual activity is essentially neither good nor evil; it is a normal biological activity which, like most other human activities, can be indulged in destructively or creatively. [But] if we take impulses and experiences that are potentially wholesome and in large measure unavoidable and

characterize them as sinful, we create a great volume of unnecessary guilt and an explosive tension within the personality. . . . A distorted Christianity must then bear some of the sexual disorder of society.

In short, self-realization is never possible when one accepts a philosophy that encourages conformity to a set of rules which run directly counter to one's true nature. It must be recognized that sexual morality requires both conviction and decision. A morality which is neither believed nor felt is no morality at all. It is for this reason that 'sexual virtue', as Wainwright Churchill observes, 'begins with the joyful acceptance of one's own sexuality and the sexuality of other people'.[21]

Summary

This chapter has dealt with those issues particularly troublesome to individuals who feel their faith is in conflict with their homosexuality: Deidre was deeply disturbed by the scriptural injunctions against various sexual practices; Lorraine expressed feelings of disillusionment with fellow Christians who failed to accept homosexuals on an equal footing with heterosexuals; Paul was once inhibited from developing satisfactory relationships with other men because of intense feelings of religious guilt; Olga internalized the sexually repressive attitudes of her parents and teachers and, in time, came to regard herself as an outcast and a sinner; Stan discussed the problems of Jewish gays in relation to a religious tradition which regards homosexual acts as 'abhorrent practices'.

Many gays have been oppressed by a condemnatory view of homosexuality which is deeply rooted in the Old Testament and perpetuated in the New. It is therefore important to remember that the Ancients interpreted their faith in terms of a tradition of sexual virtue which was preoccupied with procreation. As far as Paul is concerned, his aversion was for sexuality generally, and not simply *homo*sexuality. When we look to the ministry of Christ, we find nothing to support such an attitude, Jesus preferring to restrict his very occasional pronouncements on sexual matters to guidelines and standards for use in social relationships.

In turning our attention to the present day, we find that the churches reflect a broad spectrum of views on homosexuality. The Roman Catholic Church regards homosexual acts as always sinful, though it reserves judgement on the guilt of individual gays. A broader range of opinion prevails in the Protestant Church, while modern Jewish teaching tends to fall somewhere between the Catholics and the Protestants.

Although the churches are still far from eager to reassess the subject of homosexuality, an ever-growing number of individuals in the churches are now prepared to speak out on behalf of change and reconciliation. The question of homosexuality has already found a tentative place in the Christian agenda, and the Unitarians, Quakers, Anglicans, and others have published studies or set up working parties to explore the subject in the light of our new understanding of human sexuality.

6
Families and Friends

The death of Satan was a tragedy
For the imagination. . . .
    How cold the vacancy
When the phantoms are gone
    and the shaken realist
First sees reality.

—Wallace Stevens,
'Esthetique du Mal', VIII, in
The Collected Poems

Coming Out

'Coming out' is the most significant step in the gay person's progress towards self-acceptance. Like all important changes occurring in the life cycle of the human being, this phenomenon is accompanied by after-effects that are both pleasurable and painful. We shall consider some of these below. But, first, an attempt at definition. 'Coming out' is a term that may be unfamiliar to many readers. Even gays will often differ in their understanding, each stressing that particular aspect of the coming-out process which has proved most important to him or her. Here, then, are several definitions provided by individuals who have already been introduced to the reader in the preceding chapters:

Coming out is the realization that you're gay; it's when you begin thinking of yourself as homosexual for the first time. In a way it's like a foreign language you've been studying. You have always got to think in your own language before speaking. Then, one day, you find yourself *thinking* in this other language and, suddenly, it's no longer 'foreign' in the way it once was (**Claude**).

It's more than just telling yourself that you're gay; it's sharing this fact with other people, as you might share anything else about yourself that's important (**Lorraine**).

Coming out is the reverse of passing, which is a way of hiding yourself from others. Coming out means being as open as you are able with your friends . . . (**Nancy**).

It is having sex for the first time with someone else of your own sex (**Simon**).

Coming out implies a great deal in addition to a first sexual encounter. It's part of the whole process of self-recognition—identifying yourself as homosexual, bisexual, or whatever. And 'coming out' also demonstrates in the most positive way a willingness to involve yourself in the wider community of gay people—to be *a part of* that community (**Lydia**).

Coming out is coming of age. It's like Bar Mitzvah for the Jew, or Confirmation for the Catholic, or a boy's first pair of long trousers (**Stan**).

I would say it is a state of mind, a process of recognition. Coming out is understanding that you are part of a stigmatized minority; but it also entails a willingness to cope with the knowledge of being an outsider. I would say it is, basically, feeling positive about yourself as a gay person (**Cheryl**).

Gay people *discover* that they're homosexual. This is not the usual way of learning about your sexuality, which is a taken-for-granted thing in the life of heterosexuals. Once you can *accept* that you are different; once you can *accept* that there are people in this world who will think of you as 'queer' and a 'poof' (in other words, someone feared or hated), then you've done it! You have come out! (**Lawrence**).

In short, coming out means 'being open'. Passing, as we have seen, is a response to the stigma of homosexuality; it indicates a desire to escape negative sanctions. Coming out, on the other hand, is a courageous act of defiance, a refusal to be intimidated by the rejecting attitudes of others. But coming out is *not* the concluding chapter in a happy romance, or the proverbial sunset into which the hero rides in the final frames of a Western. Having come out, gays must still deal with all the people in their lives who will now know, but perhaps not fully accept or understand, that they are homosexual.

Coming Out at Home

Rejection by one's family is a particularly painful, and very distinct, possibility for the gay who has come out. The counsellor should bear in mind that only rarely, or if specifically told, are parents aware of their child's homosexuality. As **Alice**, Reg's mother explains:

> I always knew Reg was a bit different as a youngster; he was more sensitive than my two older boys. . . . Reg was a bit of a free spirit, really very independent, even as a small boy. . . . It wasn't until he took me aside one day and actually told me about himself that the penny dropped. It was only then that I was able to say, 'Oh, so that's what this or that was all about!'

A further explanation of why parents may not guess that their child may be homosexual is supplied by **Rita**, Lawrence's mother.

> You teach your children the same way as everybody else. You don't stop to question whether this is the heterosexual way or not. I mean, it didn't occur to me that I had any choice in what Lawry would grow up to be. . . .
> I can't truly say that I knew anything about homosexuals. Only what I picked up in the papers. I never *thought* about it, really. We never discussed it. I suppose if I thought about it at all, it was, you know, something that happened to *other* people's children. And then I might think, you know, I wonder what *they*, the parents, did wrong.

When parents do discover that a child is homosexual, their reaction is often one of 'anger, disappointment, and revulsion, as in the case of **Kay**, forty-five, the mother of Ken:

> I felt horrified, and was literally sick for days. I don't know why he's become homosexual. As his mother, I blame myself. . . .

My husband knows, and he's *terribly* against it. He feels as I do, that it's not natural. Casey, my husband, doesn't understand how people can be like that. His attitude towards Ken is just polite now. . . .

When I don't think about all this, it's all right. But it so upsets Ken to think that's he's disturbing me. And he is terribly disturbed. But as I said to him, we each have our own lives to lead. I cannot be expected to involve myself in his life, and I don't wish to. . . .

I find the sexual aspect distasteful. When I think of homosexuality I think of the sex aspect. It's unnatural. And to think that my son is involved in something so unnatural is very worrying for me, and for my husband. . . .

But we are also disappointed because we were so looking forward to grandchildren. We do feel deprived, as there are no other children. We were so looking forward to being one big family. . . .

Ken wants me to accept his friends, but I can't. I'm sorry, but I simply *can not*. . . . When I first saw him, his . . . friend, I was taken aback . . . . a seedy type, long hair, no job. He said he was a student, but I don't know. . . .

It is in relation to the family that the stigma of homosexuality weighs heaviest. The fact that gays feel unable to be open and honest with their parents is a source of great unhappiness and frustration. How odd it is, then, that in all the literature dealing with homosexuality there is scarcely any reference to the difficulties of such relationships. Even when one turns to the mass of psychiatric source material available (where parents invariably play crucial roles in the formation of a homosexual commitment), the difficulties of the gay child in dealing with parents (and vice versa) are never discussed. Yet this estrangement from the family is but one more illustration of the many ways in which *social* attitudes create the 'problem' of homosexuality. Indeed, it is in this area of parent–child relationships that the homosexual's passing lifestyle of concealment and disguise is learned and perfected. Consider the experiences of **Sandra** and **Colin**. Sandra says:

My parents think of themselves as ordinary people who, as my father is given to saying, like to 'keep 'emselves to 'emselves'. I was seventeen when I told them about being gay. I had just broken up with this girl at college. My mum sensed something was wrong, and when she asked me about it, I burst into tears and told her.

Her first words were: 'What are you *saying* to me?' She repeated that twice. Then she told my father. He came into the room and slapped me across the face. . . .

I was sent to our GP and he advised therapy. One month after telling my parents, I had my first appointment with a psychotherapist. I continued to see him on a weekly basis for the next two and a half years. . . .

I would talk a great deal about my childhood. My therapist was interested in *how* I came to be a lesbian, even though, on the surface, his attitude was that, you know, if you didn't do it in public and scare the horses, it was all right.

In reality, though, he was for ever warning me not to become emotionally involved with other girls until I was 'ready'. He never encouraged me when I mentioned any of the relationships I had formed. . . . He could be so stern in his silence. . . .

As for my parents, they kept hoping I'd be 'cured'. They also warned me against ever telling anyone about being gay. They were very concerned about what our relatives and neighbours would think . . . I'm certain this isn't because they stopped loving me in any way. It's only that they never had to think about this before—having a lesbian as a daughter.

I think they thought, at first, I had devised some cruel means of hurting them. In fact, my guess is that if you had asked them whether or not they had ever met a lesbian in their lives, they would have replied, in all honesty, that No, they hadn't.

Many parents find it extremely difficult to deal with their child's homosexuality. 'Where did I go wrong?' is perhaps the most frequently heard lament of a parent upon discovering a child's gayness. There is, in other words, a tendency for parents to think, first and foremost, of themselves. 'What are you *saying* to me?' was Sandra's mother's initial reply, followed, later, by a concern lest the rest of the family and neighbours should learn of Sandra's gayness. Given this usual pattern of response, **Colin**'s parents would appear to be a happy exception:

After I'd finished with this fellow I was deeply involved with, I wanted to tell someone who I felt cared about me. I needed a bit of sympathy. Who better than Mum and Dad?

I decided to go home for the week-end. But for two days I felt, and acted, miserable. I couldn't bring myself to say anything. There never seemed a 'right' moment when I could say, 'Well, I'm upset because I've broken up with the love of my life'. . . . I couldn't bring myself to tell the truth. Instead, I pretended I was upset because I wasn't happy with my new job. . . . Two weeks later, though, I was feeling worse than ever. So I phoned on the Thursday night and, well, I broke down on the phone. Mum said, 'What's the matter, Colin? Both your father and I know you have some problem; what is it?'

I told Mum that I couldn't tell her yet, that it was something I would have to sort out by myself. 'But we want to help you so much,' she kept saying, 'and we feel awful because we don't know how.' There was a long pause, and then she said: 'Can I ask you questions?' And without waiting for a reply, she said: 'Is it your flat?' I said that it was, but only partly. Mum was very persistent. 'And the rest?' she asked. 'Is it your feelings for someone?'

She *knew*! Because, you see, she had noticed that while I talked a great deal about my friends in London, there was one friend that I spoke about a great deal more than the others. Mum thought, as she later told me, that she guessed this was probably the first time I'd cared a lot for a boy and that perhaps I couldn't understand my own feelings. She said, too, that on more than one occasion she had given me a lead which I hadn't taken up. Over the Easter holidays, for example, she invited me to bring a 'friend' round for dinner, when, really, she had in mind this one *particular* friend of mine. But she phrased her invitation in such a way that it could have meant *anyone*. I didn't know what she had in mind, of course, so I said, 'No, there isn't anyone I'd like to bring round.'

Mum said she felt so clumsy and helpless because she knew I'd have loved to have brought him home but, well, just couldn't.

Colin feels that, though his own mother and father may be

exceptional in their ready acceptance of his homosexuality, that most gays will none the less underestimate the ability of parents to cope with the knowledge of their gayness. 'There is no doubt in my mind', says Colin, 'that I am much closer to my parents now than I was before. It's true, my dad had more difficulty in understanding, but he's come round. Perhaps not *completely*, because it's a big thing for a father to get over. But, still, we can talk to each other now whereas before we both found it a bit of a strain.'

It is perhaps even more of a strain for the parents of gays who come from a different culture than ours to accept a child's homosexuality. Ananda is Hindu, an Indian of twenty-three who has lived in East Africa for most of his life, but who came to London several years ago with his older brother, sister-in-law, and three younger sisters. His parents have returned to India, but eventually plan to settle in England. Last year Ananda joined a counsel group consisting of seven other gay people, all of whom, with the exception of himself, were born in Britain. After explaining to the group how concerned he was that his parents would discover his homosexuality, Ananda recalls that

> no one in the group understood. Maybe one person. I explained that parents have done so much for you, have sacrificed so much, have had such hopes and dreams. . . . They would be so unhappy to learn that a son is homosexual. This would be a very great shame to them.
> How can I tell them, my parents? One boy said, 'Grow up, Ananda, you're a big boy now, why should you let your parents stand in the way of your happiness? Why should you let your parents prevent you from being your true self?'
> How can I answer that? This is someone from a different world, a different culture, asking me this question. In my country, the family . . . it's different, it has a meaning, a different meaning. . . . The son marries. Then, perhaps, he goes to the home of the wife to live, as my brother did. You see? Everyone is very close together. . . .
> My brother tells me, 'In two years in England, see how Western you've become!' Maybe. If he means, how homosexual I've become, yes. But no, he doesn't know about me. . . .

It's against my religion. Homosexuality is immoral in my religion. . . . It means sleeping with many men, but caring for none. That's what they say. . . .

Someone said to me, 'Ananda, go to this pub, it's a gay pub, there will be other homosexuals. You'll make friends.' 'I don't drink', I said. 'It is against my religion.' Why should I go? What will I do? Stand around and do what?

I want one person. My love will be for that one person always. Why should I need anyone else if I love one person? It doesn't make sense to me. . . .

I still live with my brother and his family, and my sisters. We have a big house. It's nice, and I have my own room. They don't ask me, 'Where have you been, Ananda?', and questions like that. But I am close to my sister-in-law, and she says to the baby, 'When is your uncle going to introduce you to your aunt?' She means, when does Ananda get married and bring his wife home? And I say, laughing, 'Ananda will never get married.' My brother and sister-in-law always laugh at that because they are thinking to themselves, you wait, he'll meet the right one soon and then see how different it will be. I won't, but what can I do? I'm not brave. . . .

Once, a year ago, in class at college, we were talking about the law, about blackmail, and someone mentioned homosexuals. I shivered, as if I were sitting on ice, and I shouted out, 'They should kill them all! Exterminate them!' I'm so ashamed now, but I felt I must protect myself, keep the others from looking at me. They thought, after that, laughing when they said it, Ananda, he hates homosexuals. And then I felt safe. . . .

How can I tell my family? Only last week, watching television, we saw a comedian who acted like a woman, who dressed up as a woman, and my brother shook his head, saying, 'Sad people, sad people'. I left the room, thinking, he will never understand; how can I ever tell him? And what will I do when my parents arrive? They will arrive in, maybe, two years. I will not be a little boy then. . . .

How to Tell Your Parents

There is no single answer to the question of 'how to tell your parents'. The manner in which a child reveals that he or she is homosexual will depend on all the personalities involved, as well as on the existing relationship between the parents and the child. What follows, then, are only suggestions, all of which are offered by gay people who have already revealed themselves as homosexual to their parents:

It all depends on how you feel about being gay. If you're miserable about it, your parents are likely to feel the same way once you've told them. If you feel good about it, then that is also likely to affect their reactions. I told my parents at the worst possible time: when I was really depressed about things—everything, from school to pimples, to feeling lonely, to being gay. And, of course, they were horrified. Not about my skin, or my loneliness, or my bad grades, but only about being gay. Nothing else seemed to matter (**Gavin**, eighteen).

I can tell you what *not* to do. Don't tell your parents if you feel they are unlikely to understand. Don't do as I did: I folded up completely when I saw the look of shock in their faces. I'll never forget that look as long as I live. It's like a scar, now, that's never going to go away. I know that. Better that you phone and tell them, if you must, than to be unprepared for a reaction like that.
I'm still feeling very guilty because I know I am hurting them by being myself. They won't tell me this in so many words.
They won't come out in the open with their feelings. They are *so English*! Maybe if they did come out with their feelings, I could tell them how much I'm hurting inside when they act this way.
There is no understanding on their part; their minds are closed. Never tell your parents if you think they are likely to react this way. Try and prepare them first (**Mandy**, twenty-one).

You must choose the time very carefully. Don't blurt it out during an argument, because then your homosexuality becomes a weapon to wound them with, and not what it should be: something very important that you wish to share with them (**Brigid**, twenty).

What you must do is to decide whether or not to tell both of your parents or just one of them. It depends on what your

relationship is like with your mum and dad. I told my mum
first because she never flaps, and I felt she would understand.
She did understand, but she said I was right to tell her first
because father, she said, 'needs a little preparation for this'. A
week later the two of them came into my bedroom one night
and my father kissed me on the forehead and cheek and said,
'Katy, we love you now as much as ever, and we are very proud
of you for confiding in us as you did' (**Katy**, nineteen).

With my parents, I decided it was best to tell them gradually. I
knew they would be wanting to visit me at my flat, and I didn't
want to have to lie and pretend all the time about who Ruth
was, or why I wasn't dating men, or about anything else that
would mean having to deny that I am a lesbian. I began by
explaining to them that I needed to go in with another girl to
purchase the flat because of the high costs involved. Then one
evening I told them a few things about Ruth, and on another
evening I told them *quite a bit* about Ruth, so that they would
know that this was not just 'another friend'. And by the time I
actually told them about my being gay, I think they had
already guessed! (**Yolonda**, thirty-one).

If I was a counsellor, I would tell all gays who came to see me
that they should expect the worst when they tell their parents.
I would say, 'be prepared'. That is the main thing. The news is
going to surprise your parents, perhaps upset them. They will
not take it calmly. I told my parents last year, but I had
thought about telling them a long time before. I weighed the
reasons very carefully in my mind before deciding to say
anything. In the end, I felt it would be best to tell them. As I
expected, they lashed out at me. It was as if I was gay because
of something *they* did, and I was reminding them of that by
telling them. Mum said, 'You are doing this to hurt me', but
my father, he wouldn't accept it. He kept saying, 'No son of
mine is a poof' . . . (**Dan**, twenty-seven).

I don't think that anyone should force the issue with parents
or, you know, be defiant. I would not try and force my parents
to accept my girl-friends because, well, I don't think you can
force someone to change simply because you would like them
to. It takes time. When I told my mother and dad, I tried

explaining to them that I was still the same daughter as before they knew, and that maybe they could try looking at it that way (**Melanie**, nineteen).

After telling my parents I made certain that I kept the lines of communication open. I had the advantage, maybe, of reading dozens of books and articles before finally deciding to tell my parents. I also had the experience of other gay friends to work on. So I think I understood that parents have their own defences, and that my parents would have to change their ways of understanding me, and that this was not going to be easy for them. I was far more concerned about *them*, actually, than I was about myself. I felt proud of being gay, but I knew they would be unlikely to feel the same way. It was a case of my helping *them* to grow up, rather than the other way around (**Eve**, twenty-two).

What to Say and Do as a Parent

Once the parents learn of their child's homosexuality, what can they do to help their son or daughter? This is the question I put to **Ann**, Colin's mother, who replied:

It would help immensely to think of homosexuality as a kind of loving, and not concentrate exclusively on the sexual aspect of things. This was the most difficult thing of all for Mel, Colin's father. At first, he couldn't come to terms with the sex that was going on. It took a while for him to begin thinking about the sort of *relationships* that Colin might be developing. . . .

I strongly suspected that Colin was homosexual long before he ever told me. This understanding was very disturbing to me at first. A parent wants what is best for the child. As a homosexual, there are problems. You must always deal with other people's negative attitudes, even if not directed at you personally. As a consequence, life can be very difficult.

The best that parents can do for their children is to help them develop the personal resources necessary to resist the disappointments and the rejections that they will meet in life. It doesn't matter if the child is heterosexual or homosexual, you would still do the same thing. . . .

If you love your child, you love that child *as it is*. And if there is something about that child that you don't like or that you can't understand, then my advice would be to talk about it as openly as you feel able to. But *don't* put a lid on your feelings. Don't tuck your feelings away somewhere.

Some Further Advice to Parents

1. Listen to your sons or daughters as they are coming out to you. Try and discover how *they* are feeling. Most important, establish in your mind what being gay means to your children. You may well be surprised by the answer you receive.

2. Be honest in your reactions to your child's 'revelation'. If you think you may say something that you will later regret, say so. It isn't necessary to say you accept a son or daughter's homosexuality if you don't. You can say that you find it very difficult to understand; that it will be a struggle for you; that you need time to come to terms with this. *Don't hold on to your feelings*. If your child is in the least bit sensitive and intuitive, then beware lest you lose his or her trust and confidence by hiding the way you feel. *Share your feelings*—these can be a crucially important aspect of your bond together.

3. It is also important to meet your child's friends. You needn't feel obliged to *like* them. The important thing to remember is that your attitude should not be influenced by the fact that a friend happens to be homosexual. After all, so too is your child. Be as accepting as you are able, and you might learn a great deal about your child's homosexuality. You will also learn a great deal about yourself.

4. It might also be helpful to read some books on the subject of homosexuality. Be careful. So much of what has been written reflects a strong homophobic bias which is not always immediately obvious. You might, to begin with, take a look at the Critical Bibliography on p. 144.

5. Never consider the matter of your child's homosexuality closed. If you are accepting, then your child may well feel the need on many occasions to talk to you about being gay. That is what coming out is all about.

6. If there are others in the family who you feel should know,

tell them. But only tell them when the time is right. Don't rush in to tell others simply because you will feel better if others can share something that may be very heavy for you to carry alone.

7. Don't relate every little annoyance you may have with your child to the fact that he or she is homosexual. Remember, gays are no less complicated than heterosexuals, and all actions will have a multiplicity of causes.

8. Finally, and most important, let your child know that your love remains as firm as always. Remember, it took a great deal of courage, trust, and love on your child's part to tell *you*.

Coming Out at Work

The home is not the only problematic area for homosexuals who choose to be open about themselves. Discrimination in employment also means it is difficult for gays to be open at their place of work. Many employers equate sexual orientation with job performance. Thus, the homosexual—and particularly those who exhibit traits which the general public identifies as gay—will be at a disadvantage in finding and retaining employment or in being considered for promotion. It is for this reason that many gays choose to erect a heterosexual façade between themselves and their employers and workmates. When one considers that most of us spend perhaps a quarter of our working lives at our place of employment, such a passing strategy can be seen as constituting a potentially serious strain on the psychical well-being of gays.

It is true, of course, that the situation in this general area of jobs and employment is more advantageous to gays today than it was, say, ten years ago. Many more gays now feel freer to come out to friends at work, and are doing so with very positive results. Nevertheless, the hazards of being open-as-gay in one's job should not be underestimated. To illustrate this point, let us consider the position of gays in the teaching profession.

According to a recent report by the National Council for Civil Liberties (NCCL),[1] discrimination in the field of education 'rank(s) alongside the higher grades of the civil service as the area where the greatest discrimination exists'. In addition to reminding the reader of the well-publicized case of discrimination against the Inner London Education Authority teacher, John Warburton,[2] the NCCL Report cites as evidence the response it received from the 104 local education authorities in England and Wales who were sent a questionnaire designed to test attitudes towards homosexuality. Of the forty-seven replies received (only two questionnaires were actually completed and returned), approximately two-thirds of the responses were regarded by the Report's authors as 'favourable', and the remaining one-third was divided into two groups: 'confused' and 'bigoted'. Only one authority stated that it would not object *per se* to teachers being open about the fact of their homosexuality.[3]

The unfavourable replies (which were reprinted in the Report) reveal two basic assumptions prejudicial to gays: first, that homosexuals are, in themselves, a threat to children; and, second, that 'known' homosexuals are an even greater threat. (Such replies, the reader will recall, ignore the fact that gays are no more likely than heterosexuals to be paedophiles, and that a paedophile will not necessarily subject children to unwanted or violent advances.) In its conclusion, the Report acknowledges that though progress has been made since the days when homosexuality was, in itself, sufficient justification for dismissal, there still exists 'a considerable degree of prejudice' within the teaching profession.[4]

The case of **Shirley** highlights some of the problems confronting the gay teacher, and also illustrates some of the confusions of many educationists when confronted with what they regard as a homosexual 'problem'.

In February 1975 I decided to resign my teaching post at an all-girls grammar school, and I will attempt in this letter to explain the circumstances surrounding my decision.

I will begin by stating the obvious. We know that in all our schools there are lesbians on the staff who remain above suspicion by carefully hiding their homosexuality from others. They do this because they are unwilling to challenge the bigoted assumption which holds that a teacher who is known as lesbian undermines her authority in the classroom.

I do not accept this assumption. Of course, there doubtless exist students who have been conditioned to distrust or dislike homosexuals, just as there are students who have been conditioned to dislike blacks, Indians, the elderly, people with working-class, middle-class, or upper-class accents. The question we must ask ourselves is whether we should bow to such prejudices, or reject them.

Many students grow up believing that none of the people they know are homosexual. The gay image is supplied by television comedians or the uninformed and often malicious gossip of the street. Homosexuals thus come to be regarded as sick, worthless, ridiculous, criminal. Students who are gay, but who do not fully understand homosexuality, will therefore resist the truth about themselves. As a result they may feel guilty and ashamed about their feelings long after their heterosexual friends have learned to deal with their sexuality.

A teacher who is openly gay could therefore play a very positive role in the school. In eight years of teaching, the one thing I regret more than anything else is that I remained too much in the closet. You see, I too feared for my position. . . .

Of course there are many ways that we reveal the nature of our sexual orientation. Many teachers will speak informally to students of their personal lives, of their spouses, or about their children. Engagements and weddings are often discussed, in and out of the classroom. The students talk about these things, and no one ever seems unduly distressed. But could I, as a lesbian, assume the same degree of tolerance if I chose to be as forthcoming about my domestic arrangements with a female lover?

I now know that the answer to this question is 'no'. Some months ago I was discussing the Sex Discrimination Bill in my Current Affairs class. It was a lively and interesting discussion, and when the bell rang for lunch, most of the students remained behind to continue the discussion. We began talking informally about the wider implications of the Bill. One girl wondered whether lesbians would be affected. Another girl laughed at this, and said that the girl who raised this question must be lesbian herself, 'or something even worse'. A few laughed uneasily, and a flurry of comment followed.

I remained largely silent throughout. But then one girl remarked that lesbians were 'disgusting creatures'. When asked if she had ever met any, she said no, she hadn't, and explained that 'lesbians never show their faces'. No one dared to disagree with her, for they knew she would level the same charge at them: '*Lesbian!*'

It was then that I spoke out. I spoke out not because I was angry with this girl; I was not. I spoke out in order to explain what it means to live with the need to hide, to disguise, and to deny oneself. I came out to my students and told them that I was gay, but not for myself. I came out to increase their awareness, especially those in the group who might themselves be gay.

The reaction of the girls was interesting. They were not shocked or upset. They were *interested*. They were interested because my admission had made them think about certain unquestioned, *negative* assumptions about lesbians. You see, they knew and liked me as a teacher, and as a person. They were surprised, therefore, that someone they knew, liked, and respected was lesbian. They had learned something about themselves, about me, and about life. And I believe that most of them will never feel the same about lesbians again.

Several days later the Head called me to her office and asked for an explanation of my behaviour. It seems that the students had been discussing this particular class at lunch, and one of the other teachers overheard. This teacher then informed the Head.

My explanation proved unsatisfactory. I was told that I had been 'indiscreet' and that I had allowed my 'private life' and 'sexual tastes' to interfere with the professional exercise of my duties. I was also asked to give an undertaking that under no circumstances would I ever again mention or 'allude to the fact' that I am homosexual. I could not, in conscience, give such an undertaking.

I was not asked to resign, nor do I believe the Head could have forced my resignation. However, when my Current Affairs class was assigned to another teacher (ostensibly so that I would have 'more time for preparation and marking'), I felt that I no longer wished to teach in this particular school. And so I resigned. I felt then, as I do now, that there is no place for me, as a self-respecting gay woman, in an educational establishment which has made it transparently clear that it regards lesbians as a threat to pupils *in a way which heterosexual women are not.*

There are many more such cases. The general public will never hear about these. I hope that my experience will help in some small way to make the truth more available to those who are in a position to help in changing the sort of attitudes which led to my resignation.

To conclude this chapter, here is an excerpt from an address delivered in November 1973 by **Dr Howard J. Brown**, at a conference held by the Gay Academic Union of Hunter College, New York.[5] Dr Brown, who died in early 1975, was a former Health Services Administrator and Chairman of the Board of Health of the City of New York. He was, at the time of his death, a Professor of Preventive Medicine at New York University. Dr Brown speaks here of his reasons for coming out, as well as the consequences of doing so:

Seven weeks ago I got up one morning and, as usual, shut my closet door. Twenty-four hours later I had no closet door to shut; in fact the closet door had been ripped away from around me, and thanks to *The New York Times* I was the best-known homosexual in the East. . . .

I did it for political purposes. . . . I had a heart attack about eight months before I really decided to announce, and for about two days, as a physician, I knew it was possible and perhaps even probable that I might die. And I thought a great deal about the fact that you can't wait endlessly to do things. And certainly if I was going to leave some legacy to the gay cause I had to act as soon as I could. So it was really during that period that I decided it might be useful if a physician announced his homosexuality. . . .

Now I should mention that I also had some safety, though I don't think this was a central factor in my announcing. I had tenure. . . . [But] the thing that was more important to me, that gave me a greater sense of security, was that I knew the student evaluations of me were very good. . . .

I then decided that I'd ask the Public Health Association of New York City (that's an organization of public health people of which I was a member) whether they would appoint a committee to fight discrimination against homosexuals in

public health. So I spoke to the president, and went to the
board of directors, and I told them that I thought they should
pass an anti-discrimination resolution, and listed a number
of other things they could do. And then I said, 'Really, we
should appoint a chairman of the committee who's a
homosexual, and I'd like to be chairman.'
Well, there was a long pause, and there were a few
conservatives in the room that suggested a committee and a
study, but the majority came right out and said, 'No, we'll
pass the resolution, and you can be chairman of the
committee'. . . .
As many of you may know, the announcement appeared on
the front page of *The New York Times* and was followed by
some other stories in the *Times*. I appeared on every television
network in the city; and across the country I'm still getting
clippings from little towns—from front pages of little town
newspapers. . . .
The stories that were written were kind stories. . . . Across the
country the headlines weren't, you know, 'Doctor Caught as
Homosexual' and 'Doctor Announces He's Pervert', but they
were 'Homosexual Doctor Praised for His Candour' or
'Colleagues Praise Homosexual Doctor'. . . .
Meanwhile, back at the university, everyone had·to face the
fact that they had a gay professor in their midst. And the
reaction from the university has been uniformly positive.
I started out saying that I announced my homosexuality for
political reasons, and that was clearly the reason. I would now
do it for personal reasons, because I have found that I can
associate much more honestly·and clearly with the straight
faculty members. I had not realized how many things about
myself I really hid, and how many times during the day I was
still programmed to be a shadow of the way I am. . . .

Summary

This chapter has been concerned with the consequences of
coming out, a process variously defined as 'thinking of yourself
as homosexual for the first time' (**Claude**); 'sharing' your
gayness with others (**Lorraine**); 'being as open as you are able'
(**Nancy**); 'having sex for the first time with someone of your own

sex' (**Simon**); 'part of the whole process of self-recognition' (**Lydia**); 'coming of age' (**Stan**); 'feeling positive about yourself' (**Cheryl**); 'accept(ing) that you are different' (**Lawrence**).

Once gays have come out, they must deal with all the people in their lives who will now know, perhaps for the first time, that they are homosexual. Rejecting attitudes are not uncommon. These are most painful when they come from within the home. Most parents, unless specifically told, are unaware of their child's homosexuality (**Alice**; **Ruth**), and when they do discover, their reaction is one of 'anger, disappointment, and revulsion' (**Kay**), or concern about what the neighbours will think (**Sandra**). It is much less common for a parent to be accepting and helpful (**Colin**), and it may be particularly difficult for the parents of gays who come from a different culture than ours to accept a child's homosexuality (**Ananda**).

There is no single answer to the question of 'how to tell your parents', although the following suggestions have been offered: be positive about your gayness before you tell (**Gavin**); don't tell parents if they are unlikely to understand (**Mandy**); don't say anything during the course of an argument (**Brigid**); decide whether or not you are going to tell both parents or just one (**Katy**); break the news gradually (**Yolonda**); prepare yourself for the worst (**Dan**); don't force the issue (**Melanie**); understand that your parents have their own defences (**Eve**).

On discovering a son or daughter's homosexuality, a parent should endeavour to help the child develop the personal resources necessary to resist the disappointments and rejections that life may provide (**Ann**). Some further advice to parents would be: understand the importance of feelings—your child's and your own; meet your child's friends; read some books on the subject of homosexuality; never consider the matter of your child's homosexuality closed; don't rush to tell other members of the family; don't relate every little annoyance to the fact of your child's homosexuality; let your child know that your love remains as firm as ever.

Another problematic area, in addition to the home, is one's place of employment. Many employers equate sexual orientation with job performance, thus making it difficult for gays to come out at work. According to a recent NCCL Report, discrimination is particularly severe in the field of education.

Shirley's story highlights some of the problems confronting the self-respecting gay teacher, while the case of **Dr Howard Brown** reveals that the consequences of coming out to colleagues may be extremely beneficial to oneself and others.

7
Coming Together

'So here we are. Who am I? Why am I what I am? At the beginning of this book I told you how I feel about people trying to find reasons for me. I am what I am, and I fully embrace that. I am human—much to the amazement of some people.'—from *Being Different: The Autobiography of Jane Fry*, ed. Robert Bogdan

In coming out and proclaiming their true inner identity, gay people are rejecting society's definitions of them as abnormal, sick, sinners, and criminal. The guilt and shame that formerly accompanied the passing strategy of pretence and disguise is now replaced by a greater sense of pride in self. Instead of perceiving homosexuality as a failure in development, gays begin to realize the full measure of their success in resisting the overwhelming pressures of society to deny their true selves and be heterosexuals. It is thus that homosexuality ceases to be a source of guilt and shame and becomes, instead, part of a creative process of self-actualization.

Once gays have set themselves free from the tyranny of their conventional social roles, they are immediately confronted with the problems of readjustment. Part of the creative process of homosexuality consists of evolving a new basis for existing and potential relationships. Another way of putting this is to say that homosexuals, in taking the decision to come out, have chosen to relate to other people on the basis of honesty in regard to their sexual orientation. This may lead to rejection by some, as we have seen, but it also allows for the fulfilment of one's needs and desires in ways which have hitherto been hampered by the determination to pass for straight.

The 'Gay Scene'

Heterosexuals can meet other heterosexuals at any moment of the day or night. A friend, a lover, or a prospective spouse can be found at one's place of employment, at a relative's flat, at a party, in a bus queue, at college or university, in church, and so on. This is the 'ordinary' way of meeting someone. Unfortunately, though, homosexuals cannot expect to meet other homosexuals through the usual channels of social activity. This fact, which springs from society's continuing disapproval of any overt expression of homosexual behaviour, accounts for the popularity of the 'gay scene', i.e. all those public places and activities which provide homosexuals with many of their social, sexual, and psychological needs. Although the gay scene constitutes a very small corner of a much larger gay community, it none the less remains one of the few areas on the heterosexual map where gays can be certain that the people they meet and like will not be confused or angered by friendly overtures, be they social or sexual.

Critics of the gay scene (and there are many) often forget that a basic emotional need of human beings is a sense of belonging to something or to someone. It is extremely difficult to live without community. The need for identity, for the comfort and affirmation of being with others of one's own kind, is particularly intense in the case of homosexuals. Indeed, as any member of a minority group, be it political, religious, racial, social, or sexual, will testify, there are few things more satisfying than the positive reinforcement which comes from being with one's own when so many of one's day-to-day activities are shared with those who hold different views, interests, and goals. Hence, most gays, at some point or other in their lives and to a greater or lesser extent, will involve themselves in the gay scene.

The traditional gay scene consists principally of pub and club. The key fact of this world is the need for many of those who inhabit it to lead a double life. For if homosexuality were acceptable to straight society, there would hardly be the need for a scene totally apart from the mainstream. If identification with other gays in this milieu too often accentuates the negative and eliminates the positive, thereby causing intense distress for individual gays, then the counsellor will need to understand why this is so. As a partial means of answering this question, let us take a look at the gay pub, undoubtedly the central and most popular institution within the scene.

The Horse's Tail is located in an area of London best known for its bedsitters and transient population of tourists and students. The public bar of the pub (the private bar remains the almost exclusive preserve of the local inhabitants) is entered through a longish mirrored, 'modern thirties' hallway, complete with palm trees and oak panelling. The room, largely dominated by the colours blue and green, is fairly large, yet maintains a relaxing intimacy. The décor is similar to the entrance-way, with small upholstered chairs clustered around eight smallish, oval-shaped tables. At one end of the room is situated, somewhat incongruously, a 'one-arm bandit' and, at the other end, a juke-box which plays everything from pop to Puccini. Drinks are noticeably higher in price than in non-gay pubs, but this is a form of exploitation which most gays have lived with for so long that it now seems an unquestioned fact of gay life.

Ernie, licensee of The Horse's Tail, is gay. He is a large and jovial man of fifty-three, and he talks here about the changing nature of the scene in which he has lived and worked for all of his adult life:

> In the past, the gay pub was virtually the only place we could congregate, *as gays*, without revealing our 'terrible secret' to the outside world. The reason we came to the gay pub was to be ourselves. You felt a release when you walked through that door. And it was good to meet people you *knew* would be gay. Outside the pub, you could never be certain that someone who turned you on was gay or straight. You might say that visiting a gay pub avoided a lot of black eyes.
> Of course, not all gays knew where the pubs were located. We couldn't advertise. If you were a shy sort of person it might be years and years, *if ever*, before you learned of a place like this. I first discovered gay pubs through a pick-up. He asked me if I had gone to such-and-such a place, and I said no, and he gave me the address. . . .
> You'll find a lot of customers here who don't much like the 'scene', but don't know where else to go. There are people who say to me, 'It's so tense; I don't feel I fit in; no one talks to me.' They come here all the same in the hope that tonight will be their lucky night. . . .
> No one likes to be rejected. Your self-esteem is at stake. Gay

people are hassled so often that they want to be supercautious before showing interest in anyone. Look at it this way. In a place like this, your physical appearance counts for a great deal. If you're straight and you go to a dance, you go up to the girl who turns you on. It works the same way here. You go up to the person who attracts you and you start a conversation. A lot of people are afraid of being pub wallflowers, though, and this accounts for some of the tension.

One of the great myths about the gay scene is that the *only* thing that brings people to the pub is sex. This isn't true. Sex is one thing, certainly. But for many gays the pub is a place to meet friends, to chat with new people, relax, have a quick drink on the way home from work or the theatre. In other words, it's a place to be sociable with people who have similar interests. . . .

The gay club differs from the gay pub in several respects; the former requires membership, tends to be more intimate in terms of atmosphere and size and, like all clubs, is generally inhabited by a regular, if changing, core of members. **Guy** is a gay club owner, about fifty years of age. Here he talks about his club, and about certain aspects of the scene which militate against the development of personal relationships.

Our club is very small, and that gives it a feeling of intimacy, which is what I wanted. We have two bars, though, and also a juke-box, and a small dancing area. . . . The word I'd use to describe the décor is 'utilitarian'. It's comfortable. You'll notice, too, the stained glass windows, and on them are the club's initials.

One thing about this place: the people are friendly. If they're not, they won't come back a second time. The staff are pleasant, and that really creates the atmosphere. I think you've probably discovered that for yourself. You can see how friendly they are. They chat to customers, but only when they have a free moment. . . . We're very busy here from about nine in the evening till closing time. And, of course, week-ends are absolute murder!

The subscription is nominal. We only charge £1 a year. And we try to keep the prices as low as possible without actually going broke. We also try and make newcomers feel at home. A little conversation, if it's a new face, helps the person to feel more at ease. . . .

You may find the place a bit conservative, and perhaps it is. You have to remember, though, that in the old days (and my memory in the business goes back some thirty years) clubs were registered institutions. We had a committee! Everything was *impeccably* run. It was like a council meeting, really: minutes and motions, and all the rest of it. We didn't have too much interference from the police for that reason. Things were run in a very orderly way, so the police didn't interfere.

Problems? One, in particular: the vagaries of the licensing laws. One is terribly vulnerable, even though you have a club licence. The police can close down clubs more or less at will. You mentioned the Manchester club case a little while ago. Well, that's not at all unusual . . . police can enter the club in plain clothes, and if they see men dancing they may decide it's a breach of the peace. The police are entitled to use their own discretion in preserving the peace.

If you're homosexual, you can never keep yourself clean enough. That's the lesson I've learned from being in this business all these years. No matter how jolly it is in here, there's always a great deal of uncertainty, as well. And that's bad for getting to know people.

The formation of relationships on the scene can also present problems for gay women, as **Ursula**, thirty-three, explains:

Any woman who has ever stood uncomfortably on a dance floor waiting to be noticed will understand one of the principal drawbacks of the gay club as a meeting place. . . . The prevailing atmosphere is one of sexual urgency. I don't want to put the scene down. I know that for many women there is no other place to go. And clubs have the advantage of being accessible. They are there when you need them.

On the other side of the coin, the world of the club is as hidebound by etiquette as the world outside. The lines that are drawn between one woman and the next are rigidly prescribed. Even making a first move can be an incredibly complicated process. You must always ask yourself, who is the woman standing next to her—are they together? What will she expect of me? Am I her type? What do I say after I've said hello?

For a gay woman, there are two big options: 'butch' and 'femme'. When I first arrived on the scene, the pressures to identify with one or the other were irresistible. I know that roles are not so sharply defined today, but the desire to be accepted is still very great. Let's face it, a gender-defined situation is comforting, especially for women who aren't yet confident enough to relate to other women in their own independent ways.

Since the pub/club is often the point of entry into the gay scene, the young lesbian who is still uncertain of her identity and susceptible to new images of herself may find it safe to take refuge behind the comforting stereotypes of 'butch' and 'femme'. In time, though, many gay women come to feel trapped by the constricting roles they have learned. 'Thus,' say Sidney Abbott and Barbara Love, authors of *Sappho was a Right-on Woman*, 'the lesbian has two identity crises: the first is over being heterosexual or homosexual; the second, over the old but still existent choice of butch or femme'.[1]

Sexual Contacts

The gay scene, it should be stressed, does not have equal significance for males and females. The sexual marketplace character of many pubs and clubs holds less appeal for the latter than it does for the former. It is important for the counsellor to understand that the different learning and conditioning processes of men and women have resulted in certain psychosexual differences between the two sexes. Given the fact that women in our culture are conditioned to play different roles than men, sexual contacts tend to carry different meanings. For the majority of women, Ford and Beach have pointed out, 'sexual satisfaction demands more than simple genital stimulation; it usually rests upon a complex type of interrelationship with [one's] partner. . . . This simply emphasizes the fact that for the human female, physical climax in and of itself is less sufficient than it is for the male.'[2]

The social implications of these differences between the sexes are considerable. 'Among all people, everywhere in the world,' says Kinsey, 'it is understood that the male is more likely than the female to desire sexual relations with *a variety of partners*'[3] [emphasis added]. The propensity of the male (hetero- or homo-sexual) to find sexual stimulation in a greater number of situations, relationships, and things means that he is far more likely than the female to find himself in socially provocative situations. It would, for example, be very rare for a woman to cruise the streets or public toilets in search of a partner for sex; not so a man. There are lesbian clubs, as we have seen, but these are few, in relation both to the number of gay men's clubs and to the total lesbian population. In addition, gay men are far more likely than gay women to begin a potentially sexual relationship with an immediate sexual encounter.

It is also important to remember in this connection that in no two people is the intensity of the sexual instinct the same. Hence, the physical satisfaction of sexual needs may be left unsatisfied by a single partner. This is particularly true in the case of many men who, though they may enjoy the emotional satisfaction and companionship of one other person within a primary relationship, will still seek out others in an attempt to deal with their own surplus sexual needs.

'Cottaging' is, as we have seen, perhaps the most readily available means of obtaining quick and anonymous sex. If the research done by Professor Humphreys in the United States is any guide to the British situation, then it appears that a substantial percentage of the men (fifty-four per cent) involved in cottaging are married. Finding their sexual needs unfulfilled by their wives, these men find in cottaging a convenient means of obtaining sexual satisfaction without in any way endangering their primary relationships.[4]

Generally speaking, cottages are particularly well suited to men whose immediate interest is focused upon genital contacts. Of course, pubs and clubs are also available, but such places have certain crucial disadvantages: they necessitate an expense of time and money; they are very competitive in nature; they do not allow for complete anonymity. Of course, there are also gay men who, long after they have rejected feelings of guilt and shame, will continue to cottage, simply because they have learned, through conditioning and habit, to enjoy it. For such people, cottaging has two important advantages: first, it can provide sexually satisfying and emotionally non-involving encounters; second, the risks involved, though potentially disastrous to one's domestic life and professional career, may heighten the sense of sexual excitement.

From the vantage point of the 'ordinary person', it is easy to condemn cottaging. Yet such condemnation, as David Blamires reminds us, is 'more in the idea than in the reality of the act committed'.[5] Many gays who have been turned away from the mainstream of social life may find in cottaging something which cannot be found elsewhere: a temporary escape from loneliness and isolation. Such social isolation, we must never forget, is a direct consequence of the fact that homosexuals, as a minority group within society, are subject to sanctions which encourage a fragmentation of sex from the rest of their everyday lives. Such a process of fragmentation not only militates against personal happiness, but can also be damaging to one's social well-being.

If, as some critics have argued, gays are more concerned with their sexuality than heterosexuals, the reason is simply that society has chosen to regard the sexual feelings of homosexuals as a 'problem'. Fearing the penalties which might result from openness, the gay person may seek sex by furtive means. Some will make sexual contacts in cottages as a way of ensuring their anonymity. After all, if the identity of one's sexual partner is unknown, then there is no possibility of developing the relationship any further than the initial sexual encounter. In time, however, such individuals, having successfully internalized society's prohibitions against same-sex intimacy, may find it virtually impossible to respond sexually to others in a safer or more relaxed atmosphere. It is thus that the promiscuity so vociferously condemned by heterosexuals (who blithely ignore their own, leaving it to the media to reveal all the sensational details) is no more than a direct by-product of those very prohibitions imposed by society against gay relationships.

Creative Alternatives

A constructive examination of the traditional gay scene is today being undertaken by homosexuals themselves. The awakening of gay consciousness that followed the Stonewall

Riot of June 1969* has given a new impetus to the development
of a true gay community. The essential qualities of this
community are an assertion of one's gay difference and a sense
of solidarity with other gays. This gay affirmation has led to a
retreat from many of the more oppressive aspects of the pseudo-
community of the gay scene. **Glen**, thirty, speaks for many gays
when he says that, for him, 'the scene was generally a last resort
rather than a free choice':

> It isn't difficult to get hooked on the scene. It depends on what
> the alternatives are, and until recently there weren't any. So,
> no matter how much I disliked the scene, I would feel
> compelled to use it. If I wanted to meet other gays, where else
> could I go to meet them? Only the pubs and clubs.
>
> In the past it was necessary to defend the scene, if only to
> yourself. You had to preserve your self-respect. If you
> atrtacked the scene, you felt a hypocrite, because you knew
> that you'd be back there. You needed the scene, even though
> the scene didn't need you.
>
> The scene was generally a last resort rather than a free choice.
> This is why I never felt relaxed there . . . I was leading a sort
> of programmed gay life, doing things and behaving in the
> ways expected of me as a gay. It was on the scene, in fact,
> that I learned how to be gay; how to be a stereotyped gay,
> that is. . . .
>
> In the short run, the gay scene can be useful. It can be an
> important part of a gay person's coming out. Walking into a
> gay pub for the first time is a way of saying 'I'm gay', not just
> to yourself, but to others like yourself. It's like an initiation
> rite. . . .
>
> But in the long run, the scene holds you back. It's a ghetto,
> and like all ghettos it narrows your vision of yourself and the
> rest of the world. . . . What matters most in the gay scene is

* The Stonewall Inn was an after-hours gay bar on Christopher Street in
New York's Greenwich Village. On the night of 27 June 1969, the police raided
the pub over an alleged infringement of the state liquor laws. Local gays had
grown accustomed to police harassment, and could be relied upon to put up
no resistance. But on this occasion they reacted in anger, so that the police
were forced to barricade themselves inside the bar. The next evening, crowds
of gay sympathizers gathered in the vicinity of the Stonewall and protested
against the vice squad action. Within a month of the riot, the GLF was
organized and with it came the birth of the Gay Liberation movement.

being accepted—not for the person you are, but for the person you appear to be on any particular evening. It's the *appearance* that counts, and the role you happen to be playing. And if you're short on looks, youth, a good body, or the right gear, you're in trouble! This is also true of life on the commercial straight scene, but that doesn't mean gays should be the same way. . . .

I think my principal objection to the scene is that it's so difficult to get to know people. The competitive atmosphere of the pubs and clubs isn't right because it develops a spirit of rivalry, which is bad. In my own case, I remember always trying to protect myself against being rejected. I would pretend to be tough and indifferent. I'd stand there at the bar, a drink in my hand, looking around at everyone with a slightly disinterested look on my face. Like everyone else, it seems, I was determined to set up my own role from the moment I stepped into the pub.

That's the sort of role-playing the scene encourages. . . . I would say that the scene is a big obstacle to starting up a relationship, because when you're in the pub or club, you're presenting only a small part of yourself to other people. I know this for a fact, because I've had years of experience in doing exactly that. . . .

If the gay scene that Glen describes is to change, its inhabitants must first alter their perception of themselves. Those who are, like Glen, dissatisfied with the scene must first put their struggle with society into perspective. They must, in other words, define for themselves the meaning of homosexuality, and determine whether the world's view of them is consistent with the sort of people that they wish to be.

It may take a person a long time to accept the idea that such a choice exists. But it does. To begin with, one must understand something about one's basic worth, capacity, and value. The job of counsellors—perhaps their most important task—is to be of help to gays in this process of self-identification. The basic work will be done by gays. But this is not to say that counsellors cannot be of assistance in helping gays create the sort of 'inner space' which might allow for relationships to grow and develop. Developing in life is a difficult task, as people are always up against problems they have had in the past. Somebody must be there to interpret what is happening so that the troubled individual is not overwhelmed by the fact that he or she has stepped out into a bigger world where some of the same or a different set of problems exist.

Learning how to support another person is really quite difficult to do with the kind of responsibility that implies you're somehow going to drastically alter somebody's situation. But learning how to do that is what counselling is all about. People want to be happy. Usually, too, they want to trust someone. They want someone in their lives who really cares; someone who can be relied upon; someone who will be important to them. Although not everyone feels the need for a steady relationship, many of us express a desire for the companionship of another person to love and trust. Whether or not these partnerships survive depends on such factors as personality, maturity, sexual adjustment, outside commitments, and common interests. And for the gay couple one additional factor is often of crucial importance: environmental support. Gays must contend with all those social pressures which militate against the growth and development of stable relationships. The very powerful social forces which promote the stability of heterosexual unions are unfortunately nowhere present in encouraging the same stability on behalf of gay partnerships.

Jean and **Enid** are both in their early forties. Speaking of the obstacles which beset gay relationships, Jean says:

The basic problem of *any* gay relationship is learning to live with another person *as an equal*. When heterosexuals undertake to marry, each of the partners understands and accepts the role of the husband or wife. You know, the husband is the doer and breadwinner—the *active* partner; while the wife is maternal and domestic—the *passive* partner. In the beginning Enid and I emulated these roles. Of course, they didn't work. We're both very independent ladies! But we thought, you know, one of us *has to be* the 'male' and the other the 'female'. There didn't seem to be any other alternatives. So when we discovered that these roles didn't suit us, we wondered whether perhaps we were wrong for one another. . . .

Our primary problem was trying to de-condition ourselves, if
you like. We had to learn, by trial and error, the best way to
live our lives together *as equals*.

Enid agrees with Jean's assessment of the problems confronting
gay relationships, but suggests a further difficulty confronting
lesbian partnerships:

I think that a major obstacle to lesbian relationships is having
to deal with this terribly oversimplified view that people have
about human sexuality. It's true that, deep down, people
think that it's *irresponsible* for women to satisfy their sexual
needs without any accompanying desire to have a child. I find
this a very warped view of human sexuality, but it's a view that
women are always confronted with. People don't tell you this
to your face, but that only makes the matter worse. . . . Unless
gay women can resolve the problem of relating to their own
needs as lesbian women—not as society defines these needs,
but as each gay woman defines them for herself—then the
relationship is really headed for trouble.

Keith, twenty-seven, and **Charles**, thirty-one, have been living
together for the past four years. They see the problem of
establishing and maintaining a relationship from a somewhat
different perspective. As Keith explains:

I think that the main reason a lot of gay men find it difficult to
get a relationship going is that they haven't learned how to
break out of what I call 'the man's mould'. I forget who it was
that said that the woman most desperately in need of liberation is the woman every man keeps locked up in the closet of
his own psyche. And I agree with that.
I know that this certainly fits in with my own experience. I've
been learning how to 'be a man' ever since the cradle. I
learned how to be hard and forceful, competitive and
ambitious.
Most of all, though, I learned that I wasn't supposed to
express any feelings of affection for other men. I shouldn't be
tender or warm towards them. This was 'cissy'; it was 'queer'.
It's this kind of learning that makes it difficult for two men to
live together in a loving relationship. I know that for Charles
and me this has been the biggest hurdle of all—trying to

unlearn what it means to be a man. It hasn't been easy, and I don't know what will happen to us in future. Basically, I'm an optimistic person, so I think it will all come out right in the end. And if it doesn't, well, it's because you just can't change overnight; old habits die hard.

As we have discovered from the interviews in this chapter (and throughout the book), most of the gay person's problems are due to society's view of human sexuality. One problem which is rarely explored in the literature of homosexuality is the formation of 'stable relationships'. Such relationships do exist, despite society's determined efforts to put obstacles in their way. Some of these, as we have seen, are modelled after traditional marriage. But the majority are not so rigidly defined. In the eyes of the world these are often thought to be shamefully promiscuous. But such a charge is hypocritical since, in a society where passing for straight is, for many, of crucial importance, casual affairs and anonymous encounters will be easier to sustain than stable relationships. And in the absence of social supports, rules, and guidelines governing homosexual relationships, there is a strong possibility that the same stresses and strains which plague but are generally resolved in heterosexual marriage may quickly end a potentially stable gay partnership.

Jealousy is one of the most frequently cited factors in the break-up of gay relationships. In view of much current thinking on the matter which tends to identify all manifestations of jealousy with a neurotic, possessive, and insecure personality, it is important for counsellors to distinguish between those jealous feelings which spring from legitimate fears concerning the stability of a relationship, and those which might be characterized as a reflex of insecurity. It is this latter form which **Henry**, thirty-nine, discusses here:

As they say in some song or other, I was in love with love. From the moment I came out, I seemed to live in a continual state of romantic tension. I was always searching for a lifetime partner.
When I found Peter, I thought, this is IT! This is the person to complete my life! Feeling that way about him, I wouldn't let him out of my sight. If it hadn't been for the fact that he

worked on the other side of London from me, I'd have met
him every day for lunch. That's how possessive I was. I was
always worrying that he'd meet someone else. '*Who* did you
say you ate with today?' I'd ask.
Peter didn't mind at first; I think he liked the idea of my
caring about him so much. But after a while, he began to feel
stifled. At least that's what he told me. . . .
I suppose my problem was that I never believed anyone could
really love me. I was always selling myself short, measuring
myself against erstwhile or imaginary competitors. . . .
What I wanted was a relationship that would last a lifetime. I
was so concerned that Peter and I should remain together for
always that I guess, in time, I had become his jailer. . . .
In the end my constant suspicions killed the relationship. It
was all my doing. . . . I hope I've learned at least one thing
from all this, though—you can't protect yourself against
losing the one you love. I know, because the more I tried to
hold on to Peter, the less he seemed to like me. And finally I
lost him altogether.

It is often jealousy which warns us that a loving relationship is
no substitute for a lack of inner identity. Relationships can only
sustain something of their original intensity if firmly grounded
on an acceptance by both partners of the need for shared
growth. This is absolutely essential. Since the conventional
social supports inherent in the institution of marriage are
unavailable to gays, stressing the importance of independence is
crucial. It is true, of course, that independence is an intrinsically
unstable force, and it is quite possible that by growing as
individuals we may grow away from those we love. Yet in the
final analysis there is little choice but to allow for spaces in a
loving relationship—spaces in which each can help the other to
explore his or her individuality. It is out of this process of shared
growth, a sort of mutual therapy, that there develops a stability
far stronger than any externally imposed supports.

Paradoxical though it may seem, one result of deepening
emotional ties is sometimes that of sexual boredom—a waning
interest in sexual activity between the two partners in a
relationship. Assuming the continuing reality of love, this
situation is often temporary, so that genital sex is eventually

resumed. In other cases, physical affection continues in the
absence of sexual acts. To assume that this is indicative of a
failed relationship is, I feel, a mistake. Loving someone involves
a respect for the loved one's individuality, and this includes his
or her emotional and sexual requirements. Thus, if mutual
consent can be reached regarding the sexual parameters of a
partnership, there would then be little reason to fear for its
future on this account.

Those who condemn multiple relationships should not forget
the conflicts inherent in the institution of monogamous
marriage. According to psychologist Clarence Tripp:[6]

> Of the thousand or more different societies that have been
> carefully studied, less than five per cent claim to expect
> monogamy. Ours is one of them. There are no societies on
> record, including ours, that can demonstrate working
> monogamy. Where both parties, for moral or any other
> reasons, practise real monogamy, it kills the spontaneity. The
> quantity goes down, the quality goes down, and sex
> becomes routine. The non-sexual parts of the relationship
> suffer as well.

Whether gays choose multiple or monogamous relationships,
the important thing is that the choice be made in the best
interests of the relationship. Although no two relationships will
ever be the same, counsellors will bear in mind that gays are
attempting to develop creative alternatives to the socially
reinforced institution of heterosexual marriage. New
definitions of loyalty are being formulated which stress mutual
commitment to an emotional sense of responsibility rather than
simple pledges of erotic fidelity. Counsellors must therefore
encourage affirmation rather than apology, thus helping to
ensure that gays will no longer judge themselves according to
heterosexual standards of what constitutes a socially 'healthy'
pattern in their sex lives. The most important task for the
counsellor, therefore, is to help gays towards a new level of
consciousness where self-pride and social concern are united,
and where one's potential for love and human relationship can
be fully realized.

Summary

Once gays have freed themselves from the tyranny of conventional social roles, they are confronted with the problems of readjustment. Part of the creative process of homosexuality consists of evolving a new basis for relationships. But gays, unlike heterosexuals, cannot expect to meet a prospective partner in the course of their everyday activities. This fact, which springs from society's disapproval of homosexuality, explains the existence of a 'gay scene' providing homosexuals with certain of their social, sexual, and psychological needs.

The key fact of this gay scene, whose principal institutions are the pub and club, is that many of those who inhabit it feel the need to lead a double life. Obstacles to the development of personal relationships on the scene include the often tense and competitive atmosphere of pubs and clubs (**Ernie**), the uncertainty caused by the vagaries of licensing laws (**Guy**), and the rigidly prescribed roles that are frequently acted out here (**Ursula**).

Gay liberation has resulted in a reassessment of the gay scene, particularly in relation to those oppressive features which prevent gays from coming together (**Glen**). Although not everyone feels the need for a steady relationship, many do express a desire for the companionship of another person to love and trust. **Jean**, **Enid**, and **Keith** speak of the obstacles which frequently beset gay partnerships, e.g. the difficulties of two individuals living together as equals, and the pressures of society to make us all conform to pre-defined roles.

In the absence of the usual social supports, rules, and guidelines governing stable relationships, jealousy and promiscuity may operate as powerful factors in the breaking-up of gay relationships. It is therefore important for counsellors to distinguish between those jealous feelings which spring from legitimate fears concerning the stability of a relationship and those which might be characterized as a reflex of insecurity (**Henry**). It is often jealousy which warns us, first, that a loving relationship is no substitute for a lack of inner identity and, second, that the best formula for success in any relationship is the acceptance by both partners of the need for shared growth.

The most important task of the counsellor, therefore, is to be of supportive help to gays in their effort to reach a greater degree of self-realization, so that each person's capacity for love and human relationship can be fully realized.

Notes

Chapter 1

1. Alfred C. Kinsey, Wardell B. Pomeroy, and Clyde E. Martin, *Sexual Behavior in the Human Male* (Philadelphia and London, W. B. Saunders Company, 1948), pp. 610–66.
   Alfred C. Kinsey, Wardell B. Pomeroy, Clyde E. Martin, and Paul H. Gebhard, *Sexual Behavior in the Human Female*. (Philadelphia and London, W. B. Saunders Company, 1953), pp. 452–74.

2. Martin S. Weinberg and Colin J. Williams, *Male Homosexuals: Their Problems and Adaptations*. (New York and London, Oxford University Press, 1974), pp. 3–13.

3. *Counselling Homosexuals: A Study of Personal Needs and Public Attitudes*, compiled by Peter Righton. (London, Bedford Square Press of the National Council of Social Service, 1973), pp. 5–6, 31–5.

4. Christopher Z. Hobson, 'Surviving Psychotherapy', in *Rough Times*, ed. Jerome Agel. (New York, Ballantine Books, 1973), p. 173.

5. David Blamires, *Homosexuality from the Inside*. (London, Social Responsibility Council of the Religious Society of Friends, 1973), p. 22.

6. Carl R. Rogers, 'Psychotherapy Today or Where Do We Go From Here?', *American Journal of Psychotherapy*. (January, 1963), pp. 5–7.

7. Peter Wildeblood, *Against the Law*. (New York, Julian Messner, 1959), p. 32.

8. Eric Hoffer, *The Passionate State of Mind*. (London, Secker & Warburg, 1956), p. 65.

9. Jess Stearn, *The Sixth Man*. (New York, Macfadden Publishers, 1961, p. 202.

10. Weinberg and Williams, op. cit., p. 217.

11. 'Comments on *Manifesto 7*', Report prepared by the London West End Group of the Campaign for Homosexual Equality. (London, 22 Great Windmill Street, 1974), p. 18.

Chapter 2

1. Friedrich Nietzsche, *The Will to Power*, tr. Anthony M. Ludovici, in *The Complete Works*, ed. Oscar Levy, vol. 15 (Edinburgh and London, J. N. Foulis, 1910), p. 76.

2. Kinsey, *et al., Human Male*, pp. 638–9; see also Kinsey, *et al., Human Female*, pp. 468–9.

3. Ibid., pp. 474–5; see also Kinsey, *et al., Human Male*, p. 663.

4. Charles Virginia Prince, *The Transvestite and His Wife*. (Los Angeles, Argyle Books, 1967), p. 8.

5. Quoted in Arno Karlen, *Sexuality and Homosexuality*. (New York, W. W. Norton & Co., 1971), p. 367.

6. See, in particular, C. S. Ford and F. A. Beach, *Patterns of Sexual Behaviour*. (London, Methuen University Paperbacks, 1965), p. 202.
See also Karl William Kapp, *Toward a Science of Man in Society*. (The Hague, Nijhoff, 1961), p. 155.

7. See chapter 5, 'The Acquirement of Sexual Preferences', in Wainwright Churchill, *Homosexual Behavior Among Males: a Cross-Cultural and Cross-Species Investigation*. (Englewood Cliffs, New Jersey, Prentice-Hall, 1971), pp. 100–20.

8. Kinsey, *et al., Human Female*, p. 447.

9. George Weinberg, *Society and the Healthy Homosexual*. (New York, Doubleday, 1973), p. 116.

Chapter 3

1. A discussion of 'passing' in relation to group cohesiveness can be found in Weinberg and Williams, *Male Homosexuals*, chapter 13, 'Passing and Being Known About'. Also useful here is Erving Goffman, *Stigma: The Management of Spoiled Identity*. (Harmondsworth, Middlesex, Penguin Books, 1968).

2. Laud Humphreys, *Tearoom Trade: A Study of Homosexual Encounters in Public Places*. (London, Duckworth, 1974).

3. Laud Humphreys, *Out of the Closets. The Sociology of Homosexual Liberation*. (New York, Prentice-Hall, 1972).

4. Robin Maugham, *Escape from the Shadows*. (London, Hodder & Stoughton, 1972).

5. Humphreys, *Closets*.

6. Goffman discusses this passing strategy at some length in *Stigma*.

7. Humphreys, *Closets*, p. 70.

8. Dennis Altman, *Homosexual: Oppression and Liberation*. (Sydney, Angus and Robertson, 1973), pp. 58–95.

9. Ian Harvey, *To Fall Like Lucifer*. (London, Sidgwick & Jackson, 1971), p. 25.

10. T. C. Worsley, *Flannelled Fool: A Slice of Life in the Thirties*. (London, A. Ross, 1967).

11. William Aaron, *Straight: A Heterosexual Talks About His Homosexual Past*. (New York and London, Bantam Books, 1973), p. 190.

12. An excellent summary of laws which discriminate against gays, as well as the assumptions on which they are based, and practical suggestions for reform, can be found in Bob Sturgess, *No Offence: The Case for Homosexual Equality at Law*, published by CHE, SMG and USFI, 1975.

13. *Report of the Committee on Homosexual Offences and Prostitution* (The Wolfenden Report), Cmnd. 247. (London, HMSO, 1957).

14. Further comment on the anomalies of the 1967 Bill can be found in *Homosexuality: Some Questions and Answers*, published by the Albany Trust, 1975.

15. These figures are taken from the annual Home Office statistics.

16. Sturgess, op. cit., p. 23.

17. Ibid.

18. See Anna Coote and Lawrence Grant, *The NCCL Guide*. (Harmondsworth, Middlesex, Penguin Books, 1973), pp. 165–9.

19. *Questions and Answers* (unpaginated).

20. For a recent report on police attitudes on cottaging see Jack Babuscio, 'Cops and Gays', in *Gay News* No. 44 (11–24 April, 1974), p. 5.

21. Humphreys, *Tearoom Trade*, p. 160.

22. Jon J. Gallo, *et al.*, 'The Consenting Adult Homosexual and the Law: An Empirical Study of Enforcement and Administration in Los Angeles County', in *UCLA Law Review*, 13 March 1966), p. 796.

23. See chapter 13, 'Censorship', in the *NCCL Guide* for further information on the changing interpretation of the 'public good' under the law.

24. *The Guardian*, 22 August 1975, p. 9.

25. Antony Grey, 'Homosexuals: New Law but No New Deal', reprinted from *New Society*, 27 March 1969), pp. 476–9.

26. Altman, op. cit., pp. 35–7.

Chapter 4

1. See, for example, Marcel T. Saghir, M.D., and Eli Robins, M.D., *Male and Female Homosexuality: A Comprehensive Investigation*. (Baltimore, the Williams and Wilkins Company, 1973); Weinberg and Williams, *Male Homosexuals*; Humphreys, *Tearoom Trade*; H. Laurence Ross, 'Modes of Adjustment of Married Homosexuals', in *Social Problems*, Winter 1971, Vol. 18, No. 3; F. E. Kenyon, 'Studies in Female Homosexuality: Psychological Test Results', in *Journal Consult. Clin. Psychology* 32 (1968), p. 510; F. E. Kenyon, 'Studies in Female Homosexuality. VI—The Exclusively Homosexual Group', in *Acta Psychiatr. Scand.*, 44 (1968), pp. 224–37; F. E. Kenyon, 'Studies in Female Homosexuality. IV—Social and Psychiatric Aspects', in *British Journal of Psychiatry*, 14 (1968), pp. 1337–50; R. Grundlach, 'Research Project Report', in *The Ladder*, 11 (1967), pp. 2–9.

2. Goffman, *Stigma*.

3. This case was reported in *The Guardian*, 7 August 1975, p. 11.

4. Ibid.

Chapter 5

1. It should be borne in mind, however, that homosexuality was far from universally condemned in ancient times. For example, prior to the

Babylonian Exile (c. 700 B.C.), the Hebrews, as well as their neighbours, accepted homosexual activities. So also did such divergent peoples as the Egyptians, Greeks, Scandinavians, Sumerians, Carthaginians, Celts, and Cretans. 'In fact,' as Wainwright Churchill reminds us, 'certain forms of homosexuality seem to have received approval among the earliest peoples of civilization. It is precisely in the so-called cradle of civilization—the Tigris–Euphrates Valley, the Nile Valley, and the Mediterranean Basin—that homosexuality received the greatest approval during very ancient times and largely still enjoys such approval today in spite of the rise of Judaism, Christianity, and Mohammedanism.' *Homosexual Behavior Among Males. A Cross-Cultural and Cross-Species Investigation.* (Englewood Cliffs, New Jersey, Prentice-Hall, 1967; Prism Paperback edn., 1971), pp. 75–6.

2.   This point is further developed by D. Lloyd (pseud.), *Christian Renewal*, no. 10 (Summer 1973), pp. 5–7.

3.   *The Civil Law (Corpus Juris Civilis)*, ed. S. P. Scott, vol. XVI (Cincinnati, 1932), p. 288.

4.   This quote, along with a stimulating discussion of the Sodom and Gomorrah story and its impact on homosexuals, can be found in Lewis Williams, 'Walls of Ice—Theology and Social Policy', in *Is Gay Good? Ethics, Theology and Homosexuality*, ed. W. Dwight Oberholtzer (Philadelphia, Penn., The Westminster Press, 1971), pp. 163–84.

5.   It should be noted that in the Revised Standard Version (London, Thomas Nelson & Sons Ltd., 1959), the word 'effeminate' is translated as 'homosexual'. It should also be noted that the word 'effeminate' as well as the word 'homosexual' in 1 Corinthians 6.9,10 have been used in place of the term 'catamite', i.e. a prostitute cupbearer in the temple of the gods. We learn from *Strong's Concordance*, however, that catamites were not necessarily 'effeminate' or 'homosexual'. As for the phrase 'abusers of themselves with mankind', in the same passage, this is translated from the word meaning 'sodomite', which, contrary to present dictionary definitions, meant 'one who forcibly rapes another', a category which would include heterosexuals as well as homosexuals.

6.   Derrick Sherwin Bailey, *Homosexuality and the Western Christian Tradition*. (London, Longmans, Green & Co., Ltd., 1955), p. 69.

7.   Helmut Thielicke, the German theologian, argues that Paul was particularly outraged by lust, and that he did not single out same-sex relations as being any more heinous than other 'sins'; see 'The Problem of Homosexuality', in *The Ethics of Sex*, tr. from the German by John W. Doberstein. (New York, Harper & Row, Publishers, Inc., 1964), pp. 269–92. H. Kimball Jones, author of *Towards a Christian Understanding of the Homosexual* (London, Association Press, 1966), argues that the problem for Paul was one of 'sex as a depersonalizing force versus sex as the fulfilment of human relationship' (p. 76).

8.   'Historical and Mythological Aspects of Homosexuality', pp. 140–64, in Judd Marmor, ed., *Sexual Inversion: The Multiple Roots of Homosexuality*. (New York and London, Basic Books Inc., 1965), pp. 145–6.

9. These and other points are admirably argued in The Gay Activists Alliance's *20 Questions About Homosexuality: A Political Primer*. (New York, n.d.).

10. *Encyclopedia Judaica*, vol. 8 (Jerusalem, 1971), pp. 961–2.

11. 'Morality of Homosexuality', in *New Catholic Encyclopaedia*, vol. VII. (New York, McGraw-Hill Book Co., 1967), pp. 117–18.

12. See John Kane, *What is Homosexuality?* (London, Clarentian Publications, 1966).

13. Father John F. Harvey, 'Pastoral Responses to Gay World Questions', in Oberholtzer, *Is Gay Good?*, pp. 134–5.

14. Quoted from a report in *The Times*, 16 January 1976, p. 8: 'Pre-Marital Sex, Homosexuality and Masturbation Condemned in Vatican Attack on Permissiveness'.

15. *Sex and the Spirit*, no. 8.

16. *The Times*, 18 April 1973, p. 4: 'Many Clerics Homosexual, Primate Says'.

17. *The Times*, 3 June 1974, p. 16: 'Growing Church Concern with Homosexual's Plight'.

18. Lewis Williams, 'Walls of Ice', in Oberholtzer, *Is Gay Good?*, p. 182.

19. Thomas Maurer, 'Towards a Theology of Homosexuality—Tried and Found Trite and Tragic', in Oberholtzer, *Is Gay Good?*, p. 100.

20. Alastair Heron, ed., *Towards a Quaker View of Sex*. (London, Friends Home Service Committee, 1963; rev. edn., 1964).

21. Wainwright Churchill, *Homosexual Behavior*, p. 295.

Chapter 6

1. Anna Dunig, Nettie Pollard, Guy Thornton, *Homosexuality and the Teaching Profession*, National Council for Civil Liberties Report No. 8. (London, National Council for Civil Liberties, 1975), p. 2.

2. The case cited in the NCCL Report is that of John Warburton, a young temporary terminal teacher who was banned by the Inner London Education Authority after discussing homosexuality with his pupils, who had called him 'poof' and 'fairy' after seeing him on a gay rights demonstration. The ILEA demanded that Warburton sign an agreement never to discuss homosexuality with his pupils again under any circumstances, except as part of a fully structured programme of sex education. When Mr Warburton said he was not able to do this, he was banned from teaching in any ILEA school. (Report, p. 8.)

3. Ibid., pp. 4, 7.

4. Ibid.

5. Howard J. Brown, 'Coming Out', in *The Universities and the Gay Experience. A Conference Sponsored by the Women and Men of the Gay Academic Union*, 23 and 24 November 1973. (New York, Gay Academics Union, Inc., 1974), pp. 59–63.

Chapter 7

1. Sidney Abbott and Barbara Love, *Sappho was a Right-on Woman: A Liberated View of Lesbianism.* (New York, Stein and Day, 1973), pp. 94–5.

2. C. S. Ford and F. A. Beach, *Patterns of Sexual Behaviour.* (London, Methuen University Paperbacks, 1965), p. 114.

3. Kinsey, *Human Female*, pp. 682 ff.

4. Humphreys, *Tearoom Trade*, pp. 104–17.

5. Blamires, *Homosexuality*, p. 35.

6. Clarence Tripp, quoted in 'Can Homosexuals Change with Psychotherapy?', in *Sexual Behaviour* (July 1971), pp. 42–9.

Guide to Organizations Giving Advice and Help

The best way for isolated gays to learn to relate is by meeting and continuing to meet other gay people. It is only by being accepted for the person that one really is that one learns that life can hold more than rejection, indifference, and hostility. Here, then, are some useful telephone information services, counselling organizations, and gay groups which should be of interest to gays who need help in learning to relate to themselves and to other gays.

INFORMATION

The following listings should be of help to those requiring information on the gay scene—pubs, clubs, discos, coffee bars, restaurants, etc.; national and local organizations, and social groups for the sexual minorities; counselling and befriending organizations; social activities, meetings, and conferences; student gaysocs; awareness groups; gay publications, etc.

National
Gay News 'Gay Guide' (Gay News Ltd., 1a Normand Gardens, Greyhound Road, London W14 9SB). The most comprehensive, up-to-date gay guide for Britain and Ireland, the Guide is a free, monthly supplement appearing in every other issue of the fortnightly newspaper, *Gay News*; a 'Potted Gay Guide' appears in alternate issues.

National
Gay Switchboard, tel. 01–837 7324, twenty-four hours a day, seven days a week. Telephone information service based in London, but provides information on gay organizations and activities outside the London area as well.

Ashford
Kent Gay Information, 160 Faversham Road, Kennington, Ashford, Kent. Tel. 0233-25395, ext. 2.

Brighton
Brighton Lavender Line, tel. 0273-27878. Lavender People Gay Community Switchboard. Information and advice for gay women and men every Wednesday, Thursday, Friday, and Saturday, 8–10 pm.

Bristol
Gay Switchboard Information Service, tel. 0272-712621, any evening between 8 and 10.30.

Glasgow
Glasgow Gay Advisory Service, 12 Renfield Street, Glasgow G2 9AL. Tel. 041-240 1292, from 7 to 9 pm, except Tuesdays.

Isle of Wight
Isle of Wight Gay Information Service; ring Newport 5460, evenings.

London
Centerprise. Advice and information. Coffee bar. 136–138 Kingsland High Street, E8 2NS, tel. 01-254 9632.

London
BIT. Information and help service, 146 Great Western Road, W11. Open 10–1, twenty-four-hour phone service, 01-229 8219.

London
Gentle Ghost. Help, advice, and information. 33 Norland Road, W11 (2nd floor) or tel. 603 8983. Monday–Saturday, 10 am–6 pm.

London
HELP. 78 Buckingham Palace Road, SW1. Advice on abortion, VD, pregnancy testing, contraception, and legal problems. Ring Nancy or Jane, tel. 01-828 7495.

London
Wimbledon Area Gay Switchboard, 01-542 8488, Monday–Friday, 7–10 pm.

Manchester
Gay Information Centre, tel. 061-273 3725. 178 Oxford Road, M13 9RH, 7–9.30 every evening, for information on groups, gay women, gay men, transsexuals, transvestites, pubs, clubs, or just a chat.

West Midland
Gay Switchboard, tel. 021-449 8312, every evening from 7–10.

Ireland, Republic of: Dublin
Gay Switchboard, tel. 0001–764240, Thursday and Friday, 7.30–9.30 pm, Saturday 3–6 pm.

Northern Ireland: Belfast
Homosexual Information and Befriending. Write: Cara-Friend, PO Box 44, Belfast BT1 1SH.

Scotland: Glasgow
Glasgow Gay Switchboard, tel. 041-204 1292 for help and information for gay women and men every evening from 7 to 9, except Tuesday.

Wales: Bangor
Bangor Information, tel. Bangor 2075, Thursdays only, 7–8 pm.

ORGANIZATIONS

The following organizations are concerned with promoting the interests of the sexual minorities. Many of these organizations have developed social groups and activities; some have also organized counselling and befriending services, and these are listed separately below.

Albany Trust, 31 Clapham Road, London SW9 OJD, tel. 01-582 0972. Concerned with promoting the welfare of gays, principally through research and education, but it also acts as a referral agency.

August Trust. The Secretary, c/o 22 Crescent Lane, SW4. Concerned with being of help to elderly gays.

Campaign for Homosexual Equality (CHE), PO Box 427, 28 Kennedy Street, Manchester M60 2EL. Tel. 061-228 1985 or contact CHE London Office at 22 Great Windmill Street, London W1. Tel. 01-437 7363, Monday–Friday, 6–10 pm; Saturday, 2–7 pm. CHE Women's Campaign, contact Wanda Goldwag, c/o CHE Manchester, or Sue Wise 061-881 3683.
A national organization which seeks equality for homosexuals. CHE has many local groups throughout England and Wales, and is the largest gay organization in Europe. For information on the many social, befriending, and counselling services available, telephone a local CHE group or National CHE.

Friends (Quakers) Homosexual Fellowship. Contact Michael Hutchinson, 5 Brook Lane, Olton, Solihull, West Midlands B92 7EJ.

Gay Liberation Front, c/o Gay Community Centre, 78 Railton Road, London SE24. GLF Information Service, 5 Caledonian Road, London N1. GLF places great emphasis on coming out; it is not only concerned with gay liberation, but also seeks to eliminate the concepts of gender and sex roles.

Gay Wives and Mothers Collective. All women welcome. Meets monthly. Write: 39 Wardour Street, London W1V 3HA.

Irish Gay Rights Movement, Administration Office, ground floor, 46 Parnell Square, West Dublin 1. Tel. Dublin 764240 Thursdays 7.30–8.30 pm, and Saturdays 3–6 pm.

Jewish Gay Group. Weekly coffee evenings. Write to Michael Patton, 100 Shearsmith House, Swedenborg Square, London E1.

Kenric, a national non-political organization for gay women. Write: The Secretary, BM/Kenric, London WC1.

Metropolitan Community Church
Birmingham: 60 Grove Avenue, Birmingham. Tel. West Midlands Gay Switchboard, 021–449 8312.
Edinburgh: The Secretary, 1 Orwell Terrace, EH11 2DU.
Bath: University Settlement, 5 Dulcie Road, Barton Hill. Tel. Angela Needham, Midsomer Norton 413465.
Glasgow: Write: Alan R. Hunter, 1393 Dumbarton Road, Scotstoun, Glasgow, or tel. 041–954 3169.

London: Write: The Secretary, Brian Forster, 17 Balfour Road, Ilford, Essex. Tel. 01–478 6419.

National Federation of Homophile Organizations, PO Box 20, Newbury, Berkshire. Provides liaison between the various gay organizations.

National Union of Students (NUS) Gay Rights Campaign. Write: NUS, 3 Endsleigh Street, London WC1. Information about publicity for student gay societies (Gaysocs), as well as social and political activities for gay students and staff.

Nationwide Transvestite Group, TFR, 44 Monthermer Road, Cathways, Cardiff, Wales.

Northern Ireland Gay Rights Association, 4 University Street, Belfast 7.

Open Church Group is open to everyone. Write: Tom Jones, 8 Burnaby Crescent, London W4, with s.a.e.

PAL. National Paedophile and befriending and counselling organization; 'Palaver: Magazine for Paedophile Awareness and Liberation'. Box 535, 197 Kings Cross Road, London WC1.

PIE. Paedophile Information Exchange, c/o Release, 1 Elgin Avenue, London W9.

Quaker Intergroup Write: c/o Lesley Webster, 82a Christchurch Road, London SW2 3DE.

Quest, a group for Catholic homosexuals. Write: The Secretary, 8D South Park Road, London SW19 8ST.

Reach, for members of all the Christian churches. Write: 27 Blackfriars Road, Salford, Lancashire.

Sappho. Gay women meet every Tuesday at 7.30 pm, upstairs room, The Chepstow, Chepstow Place, W2. Social, disco, discussion groups, speakers.

Scottish Minorities Groups, 60 Broughton Street, Edinburgh EH1 3SA. Tel. 031-556 3673. The principal gay organization in Scotland, SMG is well established in the Scottish cities.

TAC. Write: Paula Charkin (TAC), 3 Alexandra Road, East Twickenham, Middlesex, with s.a.e. or telephone number, for free non-medical advice to male-female and female-male transsexuals.

Transsexual Action Organization, c/o The Peace Centre, 18 Moor Street, Queensway, Birmingham B4 7UH.
London Headquarters, 76 Gladsmuir Road, Archway, N19 for counselling, befriending, and information for transsexuals of both sexes and their relatives. Parents' enquiries welcome. Write: Area Organizer, or tel. 01–263 1173 Wednesdays, 8–9.30 pm.

Union for Sexual Freedom in Ireland. National Co-ordinator, Margaret McWilliam, Riversdale Cottage, Milltown, Dublin 14; National Cottage, Secretary Joseph Leckey, Vestry Hall, Ballygowan, Co. Down. Tel. Ballygowan 428.

Universal Fellowship. Write: Unifel, 16 Southside, London SW4 7AB.

Women's Liberation Workshop, 38 Earlham Street, WC1, tel. 01-836 6081.

COUNSELLING SERVICES

The following counselling and befriending services located throughout Britain are all aiming to be of assistance to the socially isolated and lonely gay person. Most provide a telephone counselling service; others enlist experienced befrienders; and several offer social facilities, as well.

National
Icebreakers. Tel. 01-274 9590 or write: BM/Gaylib, London WC1V 6XX. A nightly telephone help service for isolated homosexuals. Non-moralizing advice provided by gay men and women to callers who wish to talk about a crisis with a friend, parents, etc. Icebreakers are also quite happy to provide information on the gay scene—gay pubs, clubs, and organizations, as well as special advice, e.g. medical or legal.

National
National Friend, c/o CHE, PO Box 427, 28 Kennedy Street, Manchester M60 2EL, tel. 061-402 6750, every day, including weekends, 7.30–10 pm. A free counselling and befriending* service for gay men and women, with branches throughout England and Wales. FRIEND is closely affiliated to a number of organizations and groups, and its services are used on a regular basis by the Samaritans, the probation service, social workers, gay organizations, the clergy, and doctors.

National
Parents Enquiry, Rose Robertson, 16 Honley Road, Catford, London SE6 2HZ. An organization mainly geared to explaining to parents what it means to have a gay child, Parents Enquiry aims to demolish the myths and misconceptions that surround homosexuality.

Andover
Crisis and Support Centre, Andover 66122 any time. Counselling.

Belfast
Cara-Friend, PO Box 44, Belfast BT1 1SH.

Bradford
Friend Bradford. Tel. Cleckheaton 876 6229, evenings 6–10. Write: Friend, PO Box 47, Bradford, West Yorkshire, BD1 5YZ.

Brighton
Brighton Icebreakers, Saturdays only, 7.30–10 pm. Tel. Brighton 202930. Write: IB/Lambda, PO Box 449, Brighton BN1 1UU. Counselling.

* Befriending involves a closer personal relationship with the gay person than is generally possible for the counsellor.

Brighton
MIND (National Association for Mental Health). Counselling service for young gays and their parents. Tel. Brighton (0273) 739729 or Worthing (0908) 42069.

Bristol
Bristol Help and Information. Send s.a.e. to Confidential Friend Service, 9 Richmond Dale, BS8 2UB.

Bristol
Bristol Icebreakers. Tel. Bristol 556 925, Mondays and Fridays 7–9.30 pm, or write: Icebreakers, PO Box 86, Bath BA1 2YQ.

Cambridge
Friend Cambridge. Tel. Royston (Herts.) 41971 evenings. Write: c/o 54 Mill Road, Cambridge.

Cardiff
Friend Cardiff. Tel. Cardiff 395 123 Tuesdays 8–10 pm.

Chesterfield
Friend Chesterfield. Tel. Chesterfield 33808.

Croydon
Friend Croydon. Tel. 688 1079 Mondays, Wednesdays, Fridays 7.30–9.30 pm.

Dublin
Tel-A-Friend (TAF), PO Box 739, Dublin 4. Tel. Dublin 764240, Thursdays and Fridays 7.30–9.30 pm., Saturdays 3–6 pm.

Edinburgh
Scottish Minorities Group (SMG) Befrienders, 031-556 3673, Wednesday–Saturday only, 7–9 pm. Write: 60 Broughton Street, Edinburgh EH1.

Glasgow
Gay Christians in Scotland, Louden Connolly, 36 Chancellor Street, Glasgow WC1.

Leeds
Friend Leeds, c/o 26 Cardigan Road, Leeds LS6 3AG.

London
CENTRE. Alcoholic, legal, medical, parental, psychological, spiritual, venereal, etc., tel. 01-723 5889, Monday–Friday 7–11 pm, Sundays 3–7 pm, or visit CENTRE, Broadley Terrace, NW1.

London
Earls Court Gay Help Service. Help with practical or emotional problems, or just someone to talk to. Monday to Friday, 7–10 pm, at Nucleus, 298 Old Brompton Road, SW5. Tel. 01-373 4005.

London
Forum Gender Identity Clinic for Transsexuals. Tel. 01-385 6181.

London
Friend London. Tel. 01-359 7371 Monday–Friday, 7.30–10 pm. Write: 274 Upper Street, Islington, N1. Information on Open Counsel Groups obtained by phone or post.

London
Icebreakers, tel. 01-274 9590 every evening, 7.30–10.30, or write: BM/Gaylib, London WC1V 6XX.

London
Lesbian Counselling. Evening appointments, Monday–Friday. Tel. 01-837 1081, after 6 pm.

London
Parents Enquiry, Rose Robertson, 16 Honley Road, Catford, London SE6 2HZ. Tel. 01-698 1815, any time. Youth group, ages 15–19.

London
RELEASE. Legal, medical, drugs, abortion, etc. 10 am–6 pm Monday–Friday, twenty-four-hour emergency service on 01-298 1123. 1 Elgin Avenue, W9.

Manchester
Friend Manchester. Tel. 061-833 9602, Monday–Friday 7.30–10 pm. Write: 69 Corporation Street, Manchester M4 2DE.

Medway
CHE Medway Befriending. Tel. Medway 361049, 7–10.30 pm for advice and information.

Merseyside
Friend Merseyside. Tel. 051-708 9552, Monday–Friday 7–10 pm. Write: 14 Colquitt Street, Liverpool L1 4DE.

Newcastle upon Tyne
Friend North-East, Tel. Newcastle 841 901, 7–10 pm Fridays only Write: c/o 102 Newlands Road, High West Jesmond, Newcastle upon Tyne NE2 3NU, marking letters 'Friend N-E'.

Newport, Gwent
CHE Befriending, contact Mike, Newport 212697.

Norwich
Friend Norwich, Tel. Norwich 23285 Fridays and Sundays 7.30–10.30 pm, Saturdays 7.30–12 pm. Write: PO Box 11, Norwich NR4 7PS.

Nottingham
People's Centre, 33 Mansfield Road. Tel. Nottingham 411227 or 411676, Thursdays 5.30–9 pm.

South Yorkshire
Friend South Yorkshire. Tel. Sheffield 666 725, 7–10 pm, Fridays only Write: PO Box 107, Sheffield S1 1EJ.

Suffolk
Friend Suffolk. Tel. Stowmarket 2105 evenings. Write: c/o 7 Mill Road, Battisford, Nr. Stowmarket, Suffolk.

Sussex
Friend Sussex. Tel. Brighton 61664 Mondays 8–10 pm. Write: 9 Brunswick Square, Brighton, Sussex.

West Midlands
Friend West Midlands. Write: 161 Corporation Street, Birmingham 4, West Midlands. Call at Carrs Lane Counselling Centre, Birmingham, Thursdays 7–9 pm.

Worthing
MIND (National Association for Mental Health), counselling service for young gays and their parents. Tel. Worthing (0903) 42069 or Brighton (0273) 739729.

A Critical Bibliography

The following books are recommended to those readers who wish to explore in depth some of the issues discussed in this book.

ABBOTT, Sidney, and Love, Barbara, *Sappho was a Right-On Woman: A Liberated View of Lesbianism* (New York, Stein and Day, 1972)

A rational analysis of lesbianism from an authentic, inside perspective. The book is divided into two parts: Part One, 'What it was Like', focuses on the devastating consequences of guilt on the self-respect of lesbians; and Part Two, 'Living in the Future', reflects the new sense of pride towards which lesbians are striving, but which few, say the authors, have as yet achieved.

ALTMAN, Dennis, *Homosexual: Oppression and Liberation* (London, Allen Lane, 1974), revised edn.

Perhaps the most stimulating and insightful book to be written on the subject of gay oppression. The author describes the experience of personal liberation through self-affirmation as a homosexual, and his observations and conclusions will have relevance for all readers, regardless of their sexual orientation.

BENSON, R. O. D., *What Every Homosexual Knows* (New York, Ace Books, 1965)

A rigorous scrutiny of the four principal arguments against homosexuality ('The Nature Argument', 'The Religious Argument', 'The Psychological Argument', and 'The Non-Rational Argument'), each of which is persuasively demolished by the author.

BLAMIRES, David, *Homosexuality from the Inside: An Essay* (London, Social Responsibility Council of the Religious Society of Friends, 1973)

A brief but comprehensive look at attitudes towards homosexuality, sex roles and social pressures, coming out, and the establishment of relationships. A useful primer for young gays, as well as their parents.

BROWN, Phil, ed., *Radical Psychology* (New York, Harper & Row, 1973)

Essays on the 'myth' of mental illness, antipsychiatry, sex roles, therapeutic encounters, etc., by Thomas Szasz, Erving Goffman, R. D. Laing, *et al*. Also included here are two important gay manifestos: 'Woman-Identified Woman' and 'Gay Liberation Manifesto'.

CHURCHILL, Wainwright. *Homosexual Behaviour Among Males: A Cross-Cultural and Cross-Species Investigation* (New York, Hawthorn Books, 1967)

Churchill presents the topic of homosexual behaviour, which he regards as being within the normal range of human behaviour, in its cross-species and cross-cultural dimensions. The book is of seminal importance in the literature of homosexuality, and the chapters on 'The Acquirement of Sexual Preferences', 'Sex, Sin, and Psychiatry', and 'Sex and Morality' will be of particular interest to readers.

CRISP, Quentin, *The Naked Civil Servant* (London, Jonathan Cape, 1968)

Quite possibly the most revealing and witty memoir by a homosexual ever written. No other work so vividly conveys the feelings and attitudes of a 'self-evident' gay, or so provocatively explores the means by which society stigmatizes its sexual non-conformists.

DUFFY, Maureen, *The Microcosm* (London, Hutchinson & Co., Ltd., 1966)

A perceptive and stylishly written novel which portrays a highly credible slice of lesbian life in Sixties England.

FISHER, Peter, *The Gay Mystique: The Myth and Reality of Male Homosexuality* (New York, Stein and Day, 1972)

Dozens of answers to all the questions you ever wanted to ask about homosexuals, supplied in non-technical jargon by a gay activist.

FRY, Jane (pseud.), *Being Different: The Autobiography of Jane Fry*. Collected, compiled, and edited with an introduction and conclusion by Robert Bogdan (New York, Wiley-Interscience, 1974)

An incisive 'history' of a transsexual, told in her own words to Dr Bogdan. This autobiography is one of the most engrossing and highly readable accounts published of what it's like to be different.

GAY NEWS, Published fortnightly by Gay News Ltd. (1a Normand Gardens, Greyhound Road, London W14 9SB)

Britain's gay newspaper, providing news, a gay guide, articles on gay-related themes, short stories and poetry, arts reviews, etc. Editor Denis Lemon sets a very high standard, which makes *Gay News* an exemplary newspaper.

GREY, Antony, *Christian Society and the Homosexual* (Oxford, Manchester College, 1966)

The author is one who looks at homosexuality from the perspective of Christ's teachings.

HERON, Alastair, ed., *Towards a Quaker View of Sex* (London, Friends Home Service Committee, 1963)

The authors of this pamphlet persuasively argue that certain elements in the Church's attitude to sexuality throughout the centuries appear to be inconsistent with some of the Bible's deepest insights. Relating their observations to homosexuality, the authors conclude that morality must be creative.

HODGES, Andrew, and Hutter, David, *With Downcast Gays: Aspects of Homosexual Self-Oppression* (London, Pomegranate Press, 1974)

A passionately written and intelligently argued tract which aims to explore the phenomenon of gay oppression, i.e. a form of oppression achieved when the gay person has adopted and internalized society's hostile attitudes towards homosexuality.

HOFFMAN, Martin, *The Gay World: Male Homosexuality and the Social Creation of Evil* (New York, Bantam Books, 1969)

The research upon which this book is based was specifically designed to study those homosexuals who do not usually become the objects of scientific attention via the psychiatrist's consulting room or the courts of law. Of particular interest is Chapter 7, 'The Development of Sexual Identity'.

Homosexuality: Some Questions and Answers (London, The Albany Trust, 8a Christchurch Avenue, London NW6 1YA, 1975)

This brief pamphlet summarizes answers to some of the most frequently asked questions concerning homosexuality.

HUMPHREYS, Laud, *Out of the Closets: The Sociology of Homosexual Liberation* (Englewood Cliffs, New Jersey, Prentice-Hall, 1972)

A sociological analysis and history of the Gay Liberation movement in the USA.

HUMPHREYS, Laud, *Tearoom Trade: A Study of Homosexual Encounters in Public Places* (London, Duckworth, 1974)

A sociological study of casual sexual encounters in public toilets by a former clergyman, now Professor of Sociology at the University of Southern Illinois.

ISHERWOOD, Christopher, *A Single Man* (London, Methuen, 1964)

One of the best explorations of the gay sensibility to be found in the English novel. Highly recommended.

JAY, Karla, and Young, Allen, eds., *Out of the Closet: Voices of Gay Liberation* (New York, Pyramid Books, 1973)

A collection of personal experiences and critical essays by gays, edited by two of the contributors, Karla Jay and Allen Young, who regard gay oppression as a 'class struggle' taking place within a predominantly 'white, middle-class, male-dominated heterosexual society'.

JORGENSEN, Christine, *A Personal Autobiography*, with an introduction by Harry Benjamin, M.D. (New York, Bantam Books, 1968)

A fascinating autobiography by a transsexual whose much publicized 1952 sex-change operation awakened the world to the 'transsexual phenomenon'.

KINSEY, Alfred C., Pomeroy, Wardell B., and Martin, Clyde E., *Sexual Behavior in the Human Male* (Philadelphia and London, W. B. Saunders Company, 1948)

A scientific study of human sexual behaviour which, like its companion volume, *Sexual Behavior in the Human Female*, is unique in terms of scope, degree of objectivity, methodological skills, and interdisciplinary approach. Both studies present their evidence without moral bias or prejudice, though the authors are anxious to emphasize the significance of their conclusions to education, medicine, government, and the integrity of human conduct generally. Of special interest is Chapter 21, 'Homosexual Outlets'.

KINSEY, Alfred C., Pomeroy, Wardell B., Martin, Clyde E., and Gebhard, Paul H., *Sexual Behavior in the Human Female* (Philadelphia and London, W. B. Saunders Company, 1953)

Of special interest in this companion volume to *Sexual Behavior in the Human Male* is Chapter 11, 'Homosexual Responses and Contacts'.

MARTIN, Del, and Lyon, Phyllis, *Lesbian/Woman* (New York, Bantam Books, 1972)

The authors, both founder-members of The Daughters of Bilitis, an American gay women's organization, have been actively involved in the homophile movement for well over two decades. Their collective experiences as gay activists, feminists, and counsellors should prove useful to readers, for Martin and Lyon provide us with numerous personal and social histories.

MILLER, Merle, *On Being Different: What it Means to be a Homosexual* (New York, Random House, 1971)

A moving and often amusing account, written by a well-known author and journalist, of the consequences to his personal life and career of coming out at the age of fifty.

MURPHY, John, *Homosexual Liberation: A Personal View* (New York and London, Praeger Publishers, 1971)

This book is a statement of experiences from a new generation of gays, one which is interested in developing a sense of pride in being gay rather than passing for straight. The author's central thesis is that most of the problems confronting the gay person spring from a lack of self-identity.

Psychiatry and the Homosexual: A Brief Analysis of Oppression (London, Gay Information, 1973)

This pamphlet, the first in a series planned for publication by a collective of gay men, deals with the treatment of homosexuality by mainstream psychiatry.

RIGHTON, Peter, comp., *Counselling Homosexuals: A Study of Personal Needs and Public Attitudes* (London, Bedford Square Press of the National Council of Social Services, 1973)

This pamphlet is the published report of a working party set up in July 1970 at a national conference on social needs to study counselling services for homosexuals. Section Two is of particular interest for its practical advice on befriending and counselling groups.

ROGERS, Carl R., *Encounter Groups* (Harmondsworth, Middlesex, Pelican Books, 1973)

Practical advice on the formation and conduct of encounter groups by the founder of 'client-centred' therapy.

ROGERS, Carl R., *Client-Centered Therapy* (Boston, Houghton Mifflin Company, 1951)

The client-centredness of the Rogerian position is non-authoritarian. The 'client' is regarded as an equal, and the therapy session is known as an interview. The expression 'client-centred' indicates that the direction of the therapy process is essentially in the hands of the client rather than the counsellor.

ROSENFELS, Paul, *Homosexuality: The Psychology of the Creative Process* (New York, Libra Publishers, Inc., 1971)

Rosenfels insists that openness about homosexuality is essential to human creative development. New goals of human devotion to truth and right must emerge so that people can find a way to love and be responsible to one another out of their own human resources rather than conventional social roles.

SAPPHO, Published monthly by Sappho Publications Ltd. (BCM/Petrel, London WC1V 6XX)

A magazine written 'by homosexual women for all women', *Sappho* aims to disperse the isolation of gay ghettos via the interchange of information with gay organizations; to support all minority groups who work to counteract oppression; to encourage social groups; to relieve the loneliness of lesbians; to accept articles, stories, poems, etc.

SZASZ, Thomas, *Ideology and Insanity: Essays on the Psychiatric Dehumanization of Man* (Harmondsworth, Middlesex, Penguin Books, 1973)

This book has implicit reference to homosexuality, for the author, a psychoanalyst and teacher, warns us of the dangers of avoiding moral conflicts and social problems by defining certain behavioural patterns as forms of mental illness.

WEINBERG, George, *Society and the Healthy Homosexual* (New York, St Martin's Press, Inc., 1972; Doubleday, 1973)

Weinberg has written a powerful and persuasive treatise on homophobia, defined as an attitude of revulsion and anger towards all things homosexual.

WEINBERG, Martin S., and Williams, Colin J., *Male Homosexuals: Their Problems and Adaptations* (New York, Oxford University Press, 1974)

Drawing upon the experiences and feelings of several thousand homosexuals in three countries, the authors examine the male homosexual's problems and adaptations with respect to society's institutions, values, and stereotypes.